PIMLICO

12

COMPLETE VERSE

Hilaire Belloc (1870-1953) was born in France, of part-French Catholic ancestry, and educated at Newman's Oratory School and at Balliol College, Oxford. From 1906 to 1909, and again in 1910, he was Liberal MP for Salford. He was an active journalist, literary editor of the *Morning Post* from 1906 to 1910, founder of the *Eye-witness* (1911) and writer of innumerable essays and reviews. As well as books of verse, he wrote on religious, social and political topics; biography; history; travel; literary criticism; and novels. The best remembered of his prose works include *The Path to Rome* (1902), *Mr Clutterbuck's Election* (1908), *The Servile State* (1912), *The Cruise of the Nona* (1925) and *Belinda* (1928).

COMPLETE VERSE

HILAIRE BELLOC

With an introduction by
A. N. Wilson

PIMLICO

PIMLICO

20 Vauxhall Bridge Road, London SW1V 2SA

London Melbourne Sydney Auckland Johannesburg
and agencies throughout the world

This collected edition first published by the Nonesuch Press
1954
This revised edition first published by Gerald Duckworth &
Co Ltd 1970
Pimlico edition 1991

Printed and bound in Great Britain by
Mackays of Chatham PLC, Chatham, Kent

ISBN 0-7126-5024-5

INTRODUCTION

by

A.N. Wilson

When my biography of Hilaire Belloc appeared in 1983, it was discussed on a television programme. I watched with some trepidation, since the reviews of my book, which had been appearing in the English newspapers during the previous two weeks, had displayed a passionate hostility to Belloc – one critic stating that 'as a man, Belloc must have been about as congenial as nuclear waste', and another writing about Belloc's supposed 'malignity' in tones which would have required little modification if he had been describing Dr Goebbels. Was all this hatred inspired solely by Belloc's anti-Semitism? If so, why was not similar odium heaped on the work of Dickens, or Thackeray, or T.S. Eliot, or G.K. Chesterton, or Virginia Woolf, or Proust, by the *bien-pensant* critics? They were all writers who had written anti-semitic things, quite as offensive as Belloc at his worst. Then I began to notice that some English writers do on occasion write with positively virulent hatred of Proust; a more likely explanation of the English critics' hatred of Belloc was that he was half French.

They disliked his uncompromisingness, his disparaging view of English political systems and (often the same thing) English humbug, as of English food and English religion. They were made uneasy by his combination of political radicalism (he was the only non-socialist journalist in London who supported the General Strike of 1926) and Catholicism, which was of a very French kind – at once off-hand and belligerent. They disliked his lapidary literary style and his elegance. And all these things are more characteristically French than they are English (as was the anti-Semitism).

When the television discussion of Belloc got under way it became clear that two of the three critics had never read a word that he had written. 'Why should we take Belloc seriously?' one of them complained. And a third replied, 'Because he was very nearly a poet.'

This was actually the most damning of all the damning remarks that had been made about Belloc during that fortnight. The sad thing is, one sees what this particular critic meant. Many of Belloc's best verses are spoilt by ham-fistedness, and some of his most famous lyrics have about them a sort of boozy innocence which is not to the austere taste of the post-modernist generation. 'God be with you, Balliol men', or 'the grace of God is in courtesy', or

And there shall the Sussex songs be sung
And the story of Sussex told.

And yet Belloc the poet had a distinctive voice, without which literature would be poorer. No one else did what he did or wrote what he wrote. He is not merely a production-line Georgian.

Though he was a very funny writer, the core

of Belloc's mood as a poet is despondent. He is a man on his own in the world, as is seen in his uneven series of sonnets beginning with the words, 'The world's a stage':

> The scenery is very much the best
> Of what the wretched drama has to show,
> Also the prompter happens to be dumb,
> We drink behind the scenes and pass a jest
> On all our folly; then, before we go,
> Loud cries for 'Author' . . . but he doesn't come.

or

> The only part about it I enjoy
> Is what was called in English the Foyay.
> There will I stand apart awhile and toy
> With thought, and set my cigarette alight;
> And then – without returning to the play –
> On with my coat and out into the night.

These are possibly the best lines he ever wrote. In all his best poems he is alone, reminding me of his friend G.K. Chesteron's words, 'if we wish to depict what a man really is we must depict a man alone in a desert or on a dark sea sand. So long as he is a single figure he means all that humanity means; so long as he is solitary, he means human society. . . Add another figure and the picture is less human, not more so.'

Sometimes, in his poems, Belloc is lonely in love, and missing his wife Elodie:

But when I slept I saw your eyes,
  Hungry as death, and very far.
I saw demand in your dim eyes
Mysterious as the moons that rise
  At midnight, in the Pines of Var.

(That is a poem which, for me, passes A.E. Housman's gooseflesh test in 'The Name and Nature of Poetry'.) Sometimes the solitary voice in Belloc's poetry is homesick for childhood and for the Sussex of boyhood. Sometimes he is exuberant in his solitude, as in his mysterious song of the Winged Horse (of which there exists an excellent gramophone record with Belloc singing his own words). Sometimes, as in his epigram on 'The Telephone', he is simply lonely in town:

Tonight in million-voicèd London I
Was lonely as the million-pointed sky
Until your single voice. Ah! So the sun
Peoples all heaven, although he be but one.

It is not his most skilful epigram, but it is one of his most poignant, the more so when we remember how compulsively sociable he was. I imagine he wrote it one evening in London during his widowerhood, when he returned from a dinner to one of the rooms he rented from time to time from friends such as Charles Somers Cocks and 'Bear' Warre; and I imagine that the voice was that of Juliet Duff, with whom he was platonically in love.

He is at his best when this essentially melancholy view of life is expressed through comic means, as in his matchless 'Ballade of Hell and Mrs Roebeck' (a poem, like Larkin's 'Vers de Société', which comes into my mind every time I attend a party) or as in his epigrams such as 'Fatigue':

I'm tired of Love: I'm, still more tired of
    Rhyme.
But Money gives me pleasure all the time.

The Belloc who has perhaps travelled less well is the Georgian sentimentalist who wrote 'The Moon's Funeral', or 'Twelfth Night' or 'Duncton Hill', one of his most famous anthology pieces, marred for the modern reader by such lines as

He does not die, but still remains
Substantiate with his darling plains.

Still, while seeing these limitations, I would rather have such poems on my shelves than not.

Belloc's earliest published work was poetry and it was a poet, primarily, that he wanted to be in his early years of literary struggle when, having married young, he was trying to make a living as a professional journalist and historian. To this early phase, too, belong those verses for which he will always be remembered, the *Cautionary Tales* and *The Modern Traveller*, followed by *Peers* and *More Peers* with their marvellous BTB illustrations. The 'serious' verse is of uneven quality but the comic stuff he polished continually and it has the hard-edged surprisingness which always accompanies true poetry. The world of Henry King, who perished through his 'chief defect' of chewing little bits of string, or of dishonest Matilda whose dreadful lies led to her death by burning, or of Goldolphin Horne, who 'held the human race in scorn' and ended as the boy 'who blacks the boots at the Savoy' has a surreal quality all Belloc's own. His sentimental lyrics invite comparison with Alfred Noyes or A.E. Housman. His cautionary verses are incomparable. Children of all generations have responded to them, quite regardless of whether they themselves are ever going to move in circles where they meet the likes of Lord Lundy who spoils his chances of being 'the next Prime Minister but three' by being 'far too freely moved to tears'.

In these poems Belloc revealed what he thought of England – its crazy institutions from the House of Lords to the Fire Brigade, its social divisions, its bogus moralism. It is a farcical place where grown-ups and children alike will get into scrapes. But it is guided by no true principles, either religious or political. This total pessimism about the land of his mother's birth informed much of Belloc's historical writing and his journalism, as well as his works of political and economic analysis, such as *The Servile State*, a prophetic book, whose wisdom is clearer now than ever before. He saw Capital and Capitalism as ruining everything, and he realised that most political systems calling themselves socialist would eventually succumb to the power of Capital, because both State Socialism and Capitalism pursue collectivist solutions to human problems, and place money before soul.

In his prose works, Belloc found only one acceptable collective, and that is the Catholic Church, which he believed to provide hearth and home for the human spirit. In his poems – though there are some pious lyrics – he writes less as a Catholic than as a solitary, whose world has been wrecked.

> Ha'nacker Hill is in Desolation:
>   Ruin a-top and a field unploughed.
> And Spirits that call on a fallen nation
>   Spirits that loved her calling aloud:
>   Spirits abroad in a windy cloud.
>
> Spirits that call and no one answers;
>   Ha'nacker's down and England's done.
> Wind and Thistle for pipe and dancers
>   And never a ploughman under the Sun.
>   Never a ploughman. Never a one.

Before I began work on my biography of the man, I had assumed that this mood of solitude and desolation came upon Belloc as a result of some personal crisis in his life, such as the death of his wife in middle age, or the collapse of his faith in the Liberal Party – in whose interest he sat in the 1906 to 1910 Parliament as MP for Salford. But I soon became aware that Belloc had been an elegist before he could talk and that his sense that 'Ha'nacker Hill is in Desolation' was inborn. The outward events of his life – the early death of his father, the defeat of France by the Prussians in 1870, Belloc's failure to secure a much-coveted Oxford Fellowship, the loss of his wife, the death of two grown-up sons, the Fall of France in 1940 – all fitted into a pattern for which his imagination had been preparing him from the beginning – as did his pathetic final decade of existence.

> Life is a long discovery, isn't it?
> You only get your wisdom bit by bit.
> If you have luck you find in early youth
> How dangerous it is to tell the Truth;
> And next you learn how dignity and peace
> Are the ripe fruits of patient avarice.
> You find that middle life goes racing past.
> You find despair: and, at the very last,
> You find as you are giving up the ghost
> That those who loved you best despised you
>   most.

The man who wrote those lines cannot have been all bad. But, as I discovered when I tried to paint a sympathetic portrait of him, it is not surprising that the English did not find his presence very comforting during his lifetime; nor, thirty years after he was dead, did they much wish to be reminded of what he thought of them.

SOURCES

Books of Verse

Prose Works

Anthologies and Periodicals

CONTENTS

Sonnets

Additional Sonnet: hitherto unprinted

Additional Sonnet: hitherto uncollected

Verses and Songs

Additional Verses: hitherto uncollected

Additional Verses: privately printed

Epigrams

Ballades

Additional Ballades: hitherto uncollected

Satires, Imitations and Grotesques

Additional Verses: from miscellaneous sources

Cautionary Verses

SONNETS

SONNETS OF THE TWELVE MONTHS

JANUARY

It freezes: all across a soundless sky
The birds go home. The governing dark's begun:
The steadfast dark that waits not for a sun;
The ultimate dark wherein the race shall die.
Death, with his evil finger to his lip,
Leers in at human windows, turning spy
To learn the country where his rule shall lie
When he assumes perpetual generalship.

The undefeated enemy, the chill
That shall benumb the voiceful earth at last,
Is master of our moment, and has bound
The viewless wind itself. There is no sound.
It freezes. Every friendly stream is fast.
It freezes; and the graven twigs are still.

FEBRUARY

The winter moon has such a quiet car
That all the winter nights are dumb with rest.
She drives the gradual dark with drooping crest,
And dreams go wandering from her drowsy star.
Because the nights are silent, do not wake:
But there shall tremble through the general earth,
And over you, a quickening and a birth.
The sun is near the hill-tops for your sake.

The latest born of all the days shall creep
To kiss the tender eyelids of the year;
And you shall wake, grown young with perfect sleep,
And smile at the new world, and make it dear
With living murmurs more than dreams are deep.
Silence is dead, my Dawn; the morning's here.

[3]

MARCH

The north-east wind has come from Norroway,
   Roaring he came above the white waves' tips!
   The foam of the loud sea was on his lips,
And all his hair was salt with falling spray.
Over the keen light of northern day
   He cast his snow cloud's terrible eclipse;
   Beyond our banks he suddenly struck the ships,
And left them labouring on his landward way.

The certain course that to his strength belongs
Drives him with gathering purpose and control
   Until across Vendean flats he sees
   Ocean, the eldest of his enemies.
Then wheels he for him, glorying in his goal,
And gives him challenge, bellowing battle songs.

APRIL

The stranger warmth of the young sun obeying,
   Look! little heads of green begin to grow,
   And hidden flowers have dared their tops to show
Where late such droughty dusts were rudely playing.
It's not the month, but all the world's a-maying!
   Come then with me, I'll take you, for I know
   Where the first hedgethorns and white windflowers blow:
We two alone, that goes without the saying.

The month has treacherous clouds and moves in fears.
   This April shames the month itself with smiles:
In whose new eyes I know no heaven of tears,
   But still serene desire and between whiles,
So great a look that even April's grace
Makes only marvel at her only face.

[4]

MAY

This is the laughing-eyed amongst them all:
  My lady's month. A season of young things.
  She rules the light with harmony, and brings
The year's first green upon the beeches tall.
How often, where long creepers wind and fall
  Through the deep woods in noonday wanderings,
  I've heard the month, when she to echo sings,
I've heard the month make merry madrigal.

How often, bosomed in the breathing strong
  Of mosses and young flowerets, have I lain
And watched the clouds, and caught the sheltered song –
  Which it were more than life to hear again –
Of those small birds that pipe it all day long
  Not far from Marly by the memoried Seine.

JUNE

Rise up, and do begin the day's adorning;
The Summer dark is but the dawn of day.
The last of sunset fades into the morning,
The morning calls you from the dark away.
The holy mist, the white mist of the morning,
Was wreathing upward on my lonely way.
The way was waiting for your own adorning
That should complete the broad adornéd day.

Rise up, and do begin the day's adorning;
The little eastern clouds are dapple grey:
There will be wind among the leaves to-day;
It is the very promise of the morning.
  Lux Tua Via Mea: your light's my way –
  Then do rise up and make it perfect day.

[5]

JULY

The Kings come riding back from the Crusade,
  The purple Kings and all their mounted men;
They fill the street with clamorous cavalcade;
  The Kings have broken down the Saracen.
Singing a great song of the eastern wars,
  In crimson ships across the sea they came,
With crimson sails and diamonded dark oars,
  That made the Mediterranean flash with flame.

And reading how, in that far month, the ranks
  Formed on the edge of the desert, armoured all,
    I wish to God that I had been with them
  When the first Norman leapt upon the wall,
And Godfrey led the foremost of the Franks,
    And young Lord Raymond stormed Jérusalem.

AUGUST

The soldier month, the bulwark of the year,
  That never more shall hear such victories told;
He stands apparent with his heaven-high spear,
  And helmeted of grand Etruscan gold.
Our harvest is the bounty he has won,
  The loot his fiery temper takes by strength.
Oh! Paladin of the Imperial sun!
  Oh! crown of all the seasons come at length!

This is sheer manhood; this is Charlemagne,
  When he with his wide host came conquering home
From vengeance under Roncesvalles ta'en.
  Or when his bramble beard flaked red with foam
Of bivouac wine-cups on the Lombard plain,
  What time he swept to grasp the world at Rome.

[6]

I, from a window where the Meuse is wide,
  Looked eastward out to the September night;
The men that in the hopeless battle died
  Rose, and deployed, and stationed for the fight;
A brumal army, vague and ordered large
  For mile on mile by some pale general;
I saw them lean by companies to the charge,
  But no man living heard the bugle-call.

And fading still, and pointing to their scars,
  They fled in lessening clouds, where gray and high
Dawn lay along the heaven in misty bars;
  But watching from that eastern casement, I
  Saw the Republic splendid in the sky,
And round her terrible head the morning stars.

OCTOBER

Look, how those steep woods on the mountain's face
  Burn, burn against the sunset; now the cold
  Invades our very noon: the year's grown old,
Mornings are dark, and evenings come apace.
The vines below have lost their purple grace,
  And in Forrèze the white wrack backward rolled,
  Hangs to the hills tempestuous, fold on fold,
And moaning gusts make desolate all the place.

Mine host the month, at thy good hostelry,
  Tired limbs I'll stretch and steaming beast I'll tether;
Pile on great logs with Gascon hand and free,
  And pour the Gascon stuff that laughs at weather;
Swell your tough lungs, north wind, no whit care we,
  Singing old songs and drinking wine together.

[7]

NOVEMBER

November is that historied Emperor,
  Conquered in age, but foot to foot with fate,
Who from his refuge high has heard the roar
  Of squadrons in pursuit, and now, too late,
Stirrups the storm and calls the winds to war,
  And arms the garrison of his last heirloom,
And shakes the sky to its extremest shore
  With battle against irrevocable doom.

Till, driven and hurled from his strong citadels,
  He flies in hurrying cloud and spurs him on,
Empty of lingerings, empty of farewells
  And final benedictions, and is gone.
But in my garden all the trees have shed
Their legacies of the light, and all the flowers are dead.

DECEMBER

Hoar Time about the house betakes him slow,
Seeking an entry for his weariness.
And in that dreadful company distress
And the sad night with silent footsteps go.
On my poor fire the brands are scarce aglow,
And in the woods without what memories press
Where, waning in the trees from less to less,
Mysterious hangs the hornéd moon and low.

For now December, full of agéd care,
Comes in upon the year and weakly grieves;
Mumbling his lost desires and his despair;
And with mad trembling hand still interweaves
The dank sear flower-stalks tangled in his hair,
While round about him whirl the rotten leaves.

[8]

THE HARBOUR

I was like one that keeps the deck by night
  Bearing the tiller up against his breast;
I was like one whose soul is centred quite
  In holding course although so hardly prest,
And veers with veering shock now left now right,
  And strains his foothold still and still makes play
Of bending beams until the sacred light
  Shows him high lands and heralds up the day.

But now such busy work of battle past
I am like one whose barque at bar at last
Comes hardly heeling down the adventurous breeze;
And entering calmer seas,
I am like one that brings his merchandise
To Californian skies.

HER YOUTH

Youth gave you to me, but I'll not believe
That Youth will, taking his quick self, take you.
Youth's all our Truth: he cannot so deceive.
He has our graces, not our ownselves too.
He still compares with time when he'll be spent,
By human doom enhancing what we are;
Enriches us with rare experiment,
Lends arms to leagured Age in Time's rough war.

Look! This Youth in us is an Old Man taking
A Boy to make him wiser than his days.
So is our old Youth our young Age's making:
So rich in time our final debt he pays.
  Then with your quite young arms do you me hold
  And I will still be young when all the World's grown old.

[9]

LOVE AND HONOUR

Love wooing Honour, Honour's love did win
And had his pleasure all a summer's day.
Not understanding how the dooms begin,
Love wooing Honour, wooed her life away.
Then wandered he a full five years' unrest
Until, one night, this Honour that had died
Came as he slept, in youth grown glorified
And smiling like the Saints whom God has blest.

But when he saw her on the clear night shine
Serene with more than mortal light upon her,
The boy that careless was of things divine,
Small Love, turned penitent to worship Honour.
    So Love can conquer Honour: when that's past
    Dead Honour risen outdoes Love at last.

HER MUSIC

Oh! do not play me music any more,
    Lest in us mortal, some not mortal spell
    Should stir strange hopes, and leave a tale to tell
Of two belovéd whom holy music bore,
    Through whispering night and doubt's uncertain seas,
To drift at length along a dawnless shore,
    The last sad goal of human harmonies.
Look! do not play me music any more.

You are my music and my mistress both,
    Why, then, let music play the master here?
Make silent melody, Melodie. I am loath
    To find that music, large in my soul's ear,
Should stop my fancy, hold my heart in prize,
And make me dreamer more than dreams are wise.

[10]

HER FAITH

Because my faltering feet may fail to dare
The first descendant of the steps of Hell
Give me the Word in time that triumphs there.
I too must pass into the misty hollow
Where all our living laughter stops: and hark!
The tiny stuffless voices of the dark
Have called me, called me, till I needs must follow:
Give me the Word and I'll attempt it well.

Say it's the little winking of an eye
Which in that issue is uncurtained quite;
A little sleep that helps a moment by
Between the thin dawn and the large daylight.
  Ah! tell me more than yet was hoped of men;
  Swear that's true now, and I'll believe it then.

HER GIFT IN A GARDEN

Not for the luckless buds our roots may bear,
  Now all in bloom, now seared and cankered lying,
Will I entreat you, lest they should compare
  Foredoomed humanity with the fall of flowers.
Hold thou with me the chaste communion rare
  And touch with life this mortal case of ours:
  You're lifted up beyond the power of dying:
I die, as bounded things die everywhere.

  You're voiced companionship, I'm silence lonely;
You're stuff, I'm void; you're living, I'm decay.
  I fall, I think, to night and ending only;
You rise, I know, through still advancing day.
  And knowing living gift were life for me
  In narrow room of rhyme I fixed it certainly.

[11]

THE CHECK

Shall any man for whose strong love another
   Has thrown away his wealth and name in one,
Shall he turn mocker of a more than brother
   To slight his need when his adventure's done?
Or shall a breedless boy whose mother won him
   In great men's great concerns his little place
Turn, when his farthing honours come upon him,
   To mock her yeoman air and conscious grace?

Then mock me as you do my narrow scope,
   For you it was put out this light of mine:
Wrongfully wrecked my new adventured hope,
   Wasted my wordy wealth, spilt my rich wine,
Made my square ship within a league of shore
   Alas! to be entombed in seas and seen no more.

THE POOR OF LONDON

Almighty God, whose justice like a sun
Shall coruscate along the floors of Heaven,
Raising what's low, perfecting what's undone,
Breaking the proud and making odd things even,
The poor of Jesus Christ along the street
In your rain sodden, in your snows unshod,
They have nor hearth, nor sword, nor human meat,
Nor even the bread of men: Almighty God.

The poor of Jesus Christ whom no man hears
Have waited on your vengeance much too long.
Wipe out not tears but blood: our eyes bleed tears.
Come smite our damnéd sophistries so strong
That thy rude hammer battering this rude wrong
Ring down the abyss of twice ten thousand years.

[12]

Lift up your hearts in Gumber, laugh the Weald
And you my mother the Valley of Arun sing.
Here am I homeward from my wandering,
Here am I homeward and my heart is healed.
You my companions whom the World has tired
Come out to greet me. I have found a face
More beautiful than Gardens; more desired
Than boys in exile love their native place.

Lift up your hearts in Gumber, laugh the Weald
And you most ancient Valley of Arun sing.
Here am I homeward from my wandering,
Here am I homeward and my heart is healed.
If I was thirsty, I have heard a spring.
If I was dusty, I have found a field.

Whatever moisture nourishes the Rose,
The Rose of the World in laughter's garden-bed
Where Souls of men on faith secure are fed
And spirits immortal keep their pleasure-close.
Whatever moisture nourishes the Rose,
The burning Rose of the world, for me the same
To-day for me the spring without a name
Content or Grace or Laughter overflows.

This is that water from the Fount of Gold,
Water of Youth and washer out of cares,
Which Raymond of Saragossa sought of old
And finding in the mountain, unawares,
Returned to hear an ancient story told
To Bramimond, his love, beside the marble stairs.

★

Mortality is but the Stuff you wear
To show the better on the imperfect sight.
Your home is surely with the changeless light
Of which you are the daughter and the heir.
For as you pass, the natural life of things
Proclaims the Resurrection: as you pass
Remembered summer shines across the grass
And somewhat in me of the immortal sings.

You were not made for memory, you are not
Youth's accident I think but heavenly more;
Moulding to meaning slips my pen's poor blot
And opening wide that long forbidden door
    Where stands the Mother of God, your exemplar.
    How beautiful, how beautiful you are!

★

That which is one they shear and make it twain
Who would Love's light and dark discriminate:
His pleasure is one essence with his pain,
Even his desire twin brother to his hate.
With him the foiled attempt is half achieving;
And being mastered, to be armed a lord;
And doubting every chance is still believing;
And losing all one's own is all reward.

I am acquainted with misfortune's fortune,
And better than herself her dowry know:
For she that is my fortune and misfortune,
Making me hapless, makes me happier so:
In which conceit, as older men may prove,
Lies manifest the very core of Love.

★

They that have taken wages of things done
When sense abused has blocked the doors of sense,
They that have lost their heritage of the sun,
Their laughter and their holy innocence;
They turn them now to this thing, now to t'other,
For anchor hold against swift-eddying time,
Some to that square of earth which was their mother,
And some to noisy fame, and some to rhyme:

But I to that far morning where you stood
In fullness of the body, with your hands
Reposing on your walls, before your lands,
And all, together, making one great good:
　　Then did I cry 'For this my birth was meant.
　　These are my use, and this my sacrament!'

★

Beauty that Parent is to deathless Rhyme
Was Manhood's maker: you shall bear a Son,
Till Daughters linked adown admiring time
Fulfil the mother, handing Beauty on.
You shall by breeding make Life answer yet,
In Time's despite, Time's jeer that men go void;
Your stamp of heaven shall be more largely set
Than my one joy, ten thousand times enjoyed.

The glories of our state and its achievement,
Which wait their passing, shall not pass away.
I will extend our term beyond bereavement,
And launch our date into a dateless day.
　　For you shall make recórd, and when that's sealed
　　In Beauty made immortal, all is healed.

[15]

What are the names for Beauty? Who shall praise
God's pledge he can fulfil His creatures' eyes?
Or what strong words of what creative phrase
Determine Beauty's title in the skies?
But I will call you Beauty Personate,
Ambassadorial Beauty, and again
Beauty triumphant, Beauty in the Gate,
Beauty salvation of the souls of men.

For Beauty was not Beauty till you came
And now shall Beauty mean the sign you are;
A Beacon burnt above the Dawn, a flame
Like holy Lucifer the Morning Star,
    Who latest hangs in Heaven and is the gem
    On all the widowéd Night's expectant Diadem.

★

Your life is like a little winter's day
Whose sad sun rises late to set too soon;
You have just come – why will you go away,
Making an evening of what should be noon?
Your life is like a little flute complaining
A long way off, beyond the willow trees:
A long way off, and nothing left remaining
But memory of a music on the breeze.

Your life is like a pitiful leave-taking
Wept in a dream before a man's awaking,
A Call with only shadows to attend:
A Benediction whispered and belated
Which has no fruit beyond a consecrated,
A consecrated silence at the end.

*

Now shall the certain purpose of my soul
By blind and empty things contrólléd be,
And mine audacious course to that far goal
Fall short, confessing mere mortality.
Limbs shall have movement and ignore their living,
Brain wit, that he his quickness may deny.
My promised hope forswears in act of giving,
Time eats me up and makes my words a lie.

And mine unbounded dream has found a bar,
And I must worst deceit of best things bear.
Now dawn's but daybreak, seas but waters are,
Night darkness only, all wide heaven just air:
    And you to whom these fourteen lines I tell,
    My beauty, my desire: but not my love as well.

*

When you to Acheron's ugly water come,
Where darkness is and formless mourners brood,
And down the shelves of that distasteful flood
Survey the human rank in order dumb.
When the pale dead go forward, tortured more
By nothingness and longing than by fire,
Which bear their hands in suppliance with desire,
With stretched desire for the ulterior shore.

Then go before them like a royal ghost
And tread like Egypt or like Carthage crowned;
Because in your Mortality the most
Of all we may inherit has been found –
    Children for memory: the Faith for pride;
    Good land to leave: and young Love satisfied.

[17]

We will not whisper, we have found the place
Of silence and the endless halls of sleep:
And that which breathes alone throughout the deep,
The end and the beginning: and the face
Between the level brows of whose blind eyes
Lie plenary contentment, full surcease
Of violence, and the passionless long peace
Wherein we lose our human lullabies.

Look up and tell the immeasurable height
Between the vault of the world and your dear head;
That's death, my little sister, and the night
Which was our Mother beckons us to bed,
   Where large oblivion in her house is laid
    For us tired children, now our games are played.

★

I went to sleep at dawn in Tuscany
Beneath a rock and dreamt a morning dream.
I thought I stood by that baptismal stream
Whereon the bounds of our redemption lie.
And there, beyond, a radiance rose to take
My soul at passing, in which light your eyes
So filled me I was drunk with Paradise.
Then the day broadened, but I did not wake.

Here's the last edge of my long parchment furled,
And all was writ that you might read it so.
This sleep I swear shall last the length of day;
Not noise, not chance, shall drive this dream away:
Not time, not treachery, not good fortune – no,
Not all the weight of all the wears of the world.

*

Mother of all my cities, once there lay
  About your weedy wharves an orient shower
  Of spice and languorous silk and all the dower
That Ocean gave you on his bridal day.
And now the youth and age have passed away
  And all the sail superb and all the power;
  Your time's a time of memory like that hour
Just after sunset, wonderful and grey.

Too tired to rise and much too sad to weep,
  With strong arm nerveless on a nerveless knee,
Still to your slumbering ears the spousal deep
  Murmurs his thoughts of eld eternally;
But your soul wakes not from its holy sleep
Dreaming of dead delights beside a tideless sea.

*

O my companion, O my sister Sleep,
The valley is all before us, bear me on,
High through the heaven of evening, hardly gone,
Beyond the harbour lights, beyond the steep,
Beyond the land and its lost benison
To where, majestic on the darkening deep,
The night comes forward from Mount Aurion,
O my companion, O my sister Sleep,

Above the surf-line, into the night-breeze;
Eastward above the ever-whispering seas;
Through the warm airs with no more watch to keep.
My day's run out and all its dooms are graven.
O dear forerunner of Death and promise of Haven,
O my companion, O my sister Sleep.

[19]

Are you the end, Despair, or the poor least
   Of them that cast great shadows and are lies?
   That dread the simple and destroy the wise,
Fail at the tomb and triumph at the feast?
You were not found on Olivet, dull beast,
   Nor in Thebaid, when the night's agonies
   Dissolved to glory on the effulgent east
And Jesus Christ was in the morning skies.

You did not curb the indomitable crest
   Of Tzerna-Gora, when the Falcon-bred
     Screamed over the Adriatic, and their Lord
Went riding out, much angrier than the rest,
   To summon at ban the living and the dead
     And break the Mahommedan with the repeated sword.

★

But oh! not Lovely Helen, nor the pride
Of that most ancient Ilium matched with doom.
Men murdered Priam in his royal room
And Troy was burned with fire and Hector died.
For even Hector's dreadful day was more
Than all his breathing courage dared defend;
The armouréd light and bulwark of the war
Trailed his great story to the accustomed end.

He was the city's buttress, Priam's Son,
The Soldier, born in bivouac – praises great
And horns in double front of battle won,
Yet down he went: when unremembering fate
Felled him at last with all his armour on.
Hector: the horseman: in the Scæan Gate.

★

They that have been beside us all the day
    Rise up; for they are summoned to the gate.
Nor turn the head but take a downward way;
    Depart, and leave their households desolate.
But you shall not depart, although you leave
    My house for conversation with your peers.
Your admirable Ghost shall not receive
    Mere recollected vows and secret tears.

    But on that brink of Heaven where lingering stand
        The still-remembrant spirits hearkening down,
    Go, tower among them all, to hear the land,
        To hear the land alive with your renown.
            Nor strength, nor peace, nor laughter could I give
            But this great wages: after death, to live.

★

Of meadows drowsy with Trinacrian bees,
Of shapes that moved a rising mist among –
Persephone between the Cypress trees –
Of lengthier shades along the woodland flung,
Of calm upon the hardly whispering seas,
Of cloud that to the distant island clung –
He made of emerald evening and of these
A holier song than ever yet was sung.

But silence and the single-thoughted night,
Hearing such music took him for their own
To that long land, where, men forgotten quite,
Harpless he errs by Lethe stream alone.
He never more will know that wind-flower's white –
He never more shall hear uneasy autumn moan.

DE FIDE

[H.B. was distressed that in *The Miracle* Lady Diana
should have represented an image of the Madonna who
descends from the shrine to take the place of an erring
nun. He suspected that his objection had been exag-
gerated to her by a mutual friend.]

1

Do not believe when lovely lips report
That I lost anchor in rough seas of jest,
Or turned in false confusion manifest
To pleading folly in high beauty's court;
Or said of that you do (which in the doing
You maim yourself) what things I could not say
For dread of unassuaged remorse ensuing
On one light word which haunts us all our way.

That I grow sour, who only lack delight;
That I descend to sneer, who only grieve:
That from my depth I should contemn your height;
That with my blame my mockery you receive –
Huntress and splendour of the woodland night
Diana of this world, do not believe.

2

Believing Truth is staring at the sun
Which but destroys the power that could perceive.
So naught of our poor selves can be at one
With burning Truth, nor utterly believe.
For we that mortal are, to our derision,
Must soften certitude with that which seems,
And slake in dull repose a blinding vision,
Buy light with dark, and sleep for sake of dreams.

Mistrust, I do require you, all you trust,
And mock continuance of a steadfast mood,
And taste in all your joys their coming dust,
And call the endless flight of goodness, good.
Save in one article – Doubt earth and sea,
Doubt all that stands and is, but doubt not me.

3

Believe too little and go down despairing;
Believe too much and lose it at the end.
Believe in none and die of over-caring;
Believe in all and die without a friend.
Believe in what's to come and still go grieving;
Believe in what's gone by and find it fades.
Believe in not insisting on believing,
For all believing's but a dance of shades.

But oh! believe in me! I ask no more –
And you no more of sustenance shall need;
For that's a food ambrosial which can feed
The soul with sendings from th'Elysian shore,
As though contents eternal breathed abroad.
But don't believe in Phémé; she's a fraud.

4

Because I find foreknowledge in my soul
Of your true sisterhood with heavenly things,
And see from tardier years that further goal
Youth hides from you with its imaginings,
And witness am to your inheritance
And see beneath the passing of your grace
Un-passing calms, and a perfected face
Immutable; prefigured in a glance –

Therefore did I and therefore now complain
That you're profaned, and daily do renew
To make your own resplendent beauty vain
Through mimic beauty of what's likest you.
This was my sentence. This was all my say;
Mourning such light beclouded in a play.

5

When some great captain, French or Repington,
   Tall Seely, Townshend or Immortal Gough,
Nivelle, Maboule, Caputo, Heinrich von
   Schrifthausen, or the Portuguesian tough
That held the bridges of the Lys, but failed
   To hold them under stress of an attack,
Or Jules of the Chemin des Dames that hailed
   A passing car, and promptly got the sack . . .

When each of these with paper and with pen
   Explains the reason that he did not think,
Believe him when he boasts, believe him when
   He whines, believe him when he takes to drink.
Believe Sir Henry Judkin K.C.B.
But don't believe what Phémé says of me.

UPON GOD THE WINE-GIVER

(for Easter Sunday)

Though Man made wine, I think God made it too;
God, making all things, made Man make good wine.
He taught him how the little tendrils twine
About the stakes of labour close and true.
Then next, with intimate prophetic laughter,
He taught the Man, in His own image blest,
To pluck and waggon and to – all the rest!
To tread the grape and work his vintage after.

So did God make us, making good wine's makers;
So did he order us to rule the field.
And now by God are we not only bakers
But vintners also, sacraments to yield;
Yet most of all strong lovers. Praised be God!
Who taught us how the wine-press should be trod.

VERSES AND SONGS

THE NIGHT

Most holy Night, that still dost keep
The keys of all the doors of sleep,
To me when my tired eyelids close
    Give thou repose.

And let the far lament of them
That chaunt the dead day's requiem
Make in my ears, who wakeful lie,
    Soft lullaby.

Let them that guard the hornéd moon
By my bedside their memories croon.
So shall I have new dreams and blest
    In my brief rest.

Fold your great wings about my face,
Hide dawning from my resting-place,
And cheat me with your false delight,
    Most holy Night.

HOMAGE

There is a light around your head
Which only Saints of God may wear,
And all the flowers on which you tread
In plesaunce more than ours have fed,
And supped the essential air
Whose summer is a-pulse with music everywhere.

For you are younger than the mornings are
That in the mountains break;
When upland shepherds see their only star
Pale on the dawn, and make
In his surcease the hours,
The early hours of all their happy circuit take.

[29]

CUCKOO!

In woods so long time bare.
        Cuckoo!
Up and in the wood, I know not where,
Two notes fall.
Yet I do not envy him at all
His phantasy.
Cuckoo!
I too,
Somewhere,
I have sung as merrily as he
Who can dare,
Small and careless lover, so to laugh at care,
And who
Can call
Cuckoo!
In woods of winter weary,
In scented woods, of winter weary, call
Cuckoo!
In woods so long time bare.

NOËL

On a winter's night long time ago
    (*The bells ring loud and the bells ring low*),
When high howled wind, and down fell snow
    (Carillon, Carilla),
Saint Joseph he and Nostre Dame,
Riding on an ass, full weary came
From Nazareth into Bethlehem.
    And the small child Jesus smile on you.

And Bethlehem inn they stood before
    (*The bells ring less and the bells ring more*),
The landlord bade them begone from his door
    (Carillon, Carilla).
'Poor folk' (says he) 'must lie where they may,
For the Duke of Jewry comes this way,
With all his train on a Christmas Day.'
    And the small child Jesus smile on you.

Poor folk that may my carol hear
    (*The bells ring single and the bells ring clear*),
See! God's one child had hardest cheer!
    (Carillon, Carilla).
Men grown hard on a Christmas morn;
The dumb beast by and a babe forlorn.
It was very, very cold when our Lord was born.
    And the small child Jesus smile on you.

Now these were Jews as Jews must be
    (*The bells ring merry and the bells ring free*).
But Christian men in a band are we
    (Carillon, Carilla).
Empty we go, and ill bedight,
Singing Noël on a winter's night.
Give us to sup by the warm firelight.
    And the small child Jesus smile on you.

THE EARLY MORNING

The moon on the one hand, the dawn on the other:
The moon is my sister, the dawn is my brother.
The moon on my left and the dawn on my right.
My brother, good morning: my sister, good night.

[31]

AUVERGNAT

There was a man was half a clown
(It's so my father tells of it).
He saw the church in Clermont town
And laughed to hear the bells of it.

He laughed to hear the bells that ring
In Clermont Church and round of it;
He heard the verger's daughter sing,
And loved her for the sound of it.

The verger's daughter said him nay;
She had the right of choice in it.
He left the town at break of day:
He hadn't had a voice in it.

The road went up, the road went down,
And there the matter ended it.
He broke his heart in Clermont town,
At Pontgibaud they mended it.

THE WORLD'S END

The clouds are high and the skies are wide
  (*It's a weary way to the world's end*).
I hear the wind upon a hillside
  (*Over the hills, away*).

Over the hills and over the sea
  (*It's a weary way to the world's end*).
The woman alone is a-calling me
  (*Over the hills, away*).

Beyond the rim of the rising moon
  (*It's a weary way to the world's end*).
He's back too late who starts too soon
  (*Over the hills, away*).

[32]

He's wise and he laughs who loves to roam
  (*It's a weary way to the world's end*);
He's wise and he cries the when he comes home
  (*Over the hills, away*).

Woman alone, and all alone
  (*It's a weary way to the world's end*).
I'll just be sitting at home, my own,
  The world's a weary way.

FILLE-LA-HAINE

Death went into the steeple to ring,
  And he pulled the rope and he tolled a knell.
Fille-la-Haine, how well you sing!
  Why are they ringing the Passing Bell?
Death went into the steeple to ring;
Fille-la-Haine, how well you sing!

Death went down the stream in a boat,
  Down the river of Seine went he;
Fille-la-Haine had a pain in her throat,
  Fille-la-Haine was nothing to me.
Death went down the stream in a boat;
Fille-la-Haine had a pain in her throat.

Death went up the hill in a cart
  (I have forgotten her lips and her laughter).
Fille-la-Haine was my sweetheart
  (And all the village was following after).
Death went up the hill in a cart;
Fille-la-Haine was my sweetheart.

The Moon is dead. I saw her die.
She in a drifting cloud was drest,
She lay along the uncertain west,
A dream to see.
And very low she spake to me:
'I go where none may understand,
I fade into the nameless land,
And there must lie perpetually.'
And therefore I,
And therefore loudly, loudly I
And high
And very piteously make cry:
'The Moon is dead. I saw her die.'

And will she never rise again?
The Holy Moon? Oh, never more!
Perhaps along the inhuman shore
Where pale ghosts are
Beyond the low lethean fen
She and some wide infernal star . . .
To us who loved her never more,
The Moon will never rise again.
Oh! never more in nightly sky
Her eye so high shall peep and pry
To see the great world rolling by.
For why?
The Moon is dead. I saw her die.

The woods and downs have caught the mid-December,
   The noisy woods and high sea-downs of home;
The wind has found me and I do remember
   The strong scent of the foam.

Woods, darlings of my wandering feet, another
   Possesses you, another treads the Down;
The South West Wind that was my elder brother
   Has come to me in town.

The wind is shouting from the hills of morning,
   I do remember and I will not stay.
I'll take the Hampton road without a warning
   And get me clean away.

The channel is up, the little seas are leaping,
   The tide is making over Arun Bar;
And there's my boat, where all the rest are sleeping
   And my companions are.

I'll board her, and apparel her, and I'll mount her,
   My boat, that was the strongest friend to me –
That brought my boyhood to its first encounter
   And taught me the wide sea.

Now shall I drive her, roaring hard a' weather,
   Right for the salt and leave them all behind;
We'll quite forget the treacherous streets together
   And find – or shall we find?

There is no Pilotry my soul relies on
   Whereby to catch beneath my bended hand,
Faint and beloved along the extreme horizon,
   That unforgotten land.

We shall not round the granite piers and paven
   To lie to wharves we know with canvas furled.
My little Boat, we shall not make the haven –
   It is not of the world.

Somewhere of English forelands grandly guarded
   It stands, but not for exiles, marked and clean;
Oh! not for us. A mist has risen and marred it: –
   My youth lies in between.

So in this snare that holds me and appals me,
   Where honour hardly lives nor loves remain,
The Sea compels me and my County calls me,
   But stronger things restrain.

                    .   .   .

England, to me that never have malingered,
   Nor spoken falsely, nor your flattery used,
Nor even in my rightful garden lingered: –
   What have you not refused?

THE SOUTH COUNTRY

When I am living in the Midlands
   That are sodden and unkind,
I light my lamp in the evening:
   My work is left behind;
And the great hills of the South Country
   Come back into my mind.

The great hills of the South Country
   They stand along the sea;
And it's there walking in the high woods
   That I could wish to be,
And the men that were boys when I was a boy
   Walking along with me.

The men that live in North England
    I saw them for a day:
Their hearts are set upon the waste fells,
    Their skies are fast and grey;
From their castle-walls a man may see
    The mountains far away.

The men that live in West England
    They see the Severn strong,
A-rolling on rough water brown
    Light aspen leaves along.
They have the secret of the Rocks,
    And the oldest kind of song.

But the men that live in the South Country
    Are the kindest and most wise,
They get their laughter from the loud surf,
    And the faith in their happy eyes
Comes surely from our Sister the Spring
    When over the sea she flies;
The violets suddenly bloom at her feet,
    She blesses us with surprise.

I never get between the pines
    But I smell the Sussex air;
Nor I never come on a belt of sand
    But my home is there.
And along the sky the line of the Downs
    So noble and so bare.

A lost thing could I never find,
    Nor a broken thing mend:
And I fear I shall be all alone
    When I get towards the end.

Who will there be to comfort me
    Or who will be my friend?

I will gather and carefully make my friends
    Of the men of the Sussex Weald,
They watch the stars from silent folds,
    They stiffly plough the field.
By them and the God of the South Country
    My poor soul shall be healed.

If I ever become a rich man,
    Or if ever I grow to be old,
I will build a house with deep thatch
    To shelter me from the cold,
And there shall the Sussex songs be sung
    And the story of Sussex told.

I will hold my house in the high wood
    Within a walk of the sea,
And the men that were boys when I was a boy
    Shall sit and drink with me.

THE BIRDS

When Jesus Christ was four years old,
The angels brought Him toys of gold,
Which no man ever had bought or sold.

And yet with these He would not play.
He made Him small fowl out of clay,
And blessed them till they flew away:
    Tu creasti Domine.

Jesus Christ, Thou child so wise,
Bless mine hands and fill mine eyes,
And bring my soul to Paradise.

[38]

They warned Our Lady for the Child
   That was Our blessed Lord,
And She took Him into the desert wild,
   Over the camel's ford.

And a long song She sang to Him
   And a short story told:
And She wrapped Him in a woollen cloak
   To keep Him from the cold.

But when Our Lord was grown a man
   The Rich they dragged Him down,
And they crucified Him in Golgotha,
   Out and beyond the Town.

They crucified Him on Calvary,
   Upon an April day;
And because He had been her little Son
   She followed Him all the way.

Our Lady stood beside the Cross,
   A little space apart,
And when She heard Our Lord cry out
   A sword went through Her Heart.

They laid Our Lord in a marble tomb,
   Dead, in a winding sheet.
But Our Lady stands above the world
   With the white Moon at Her feet.

IN A BOAT

Lady! Lady!
Upon Heaven-height,
Above the harsh morning
In the mere light.

[39]

Above the spindrift
And above the snow,
Where no seas tumble,
And no winds blow.

The twisting tides
And the perilous sands
Upon all sides
Are in your holy hands.

The wind harries
And the cold kills;
But I see your chapel
Over far hills.

My body is frozen,
My soul is afraid:
Stretch out your hands to me,
Mother and maid.

Mother of Christ,
And Mother of me,
Save me alive
From the howl of the sea.

If you will Mother me
Till I grow old,
I will hang in your chapel
A ship of pure gold.

COURTESY

Of Courtesy, it is much less
Than Courage of Heart or Holiness,
Yet in my Walks it seems to me
That the Grace of God is in Courtesy.

On Monks I did in Storrington fall,
They took me straight into their Hall;
I saw Three Pictures on a wall,
And Courtesy was in them all.

The first the Annunciation;
The second the Visitation;
The third the Consolation,
Of God that was Our Lady's Son.

The first was of Saint Gabriel;
On Wings a-flame from Heaven he fell;
And as he went upon one knee
He shone with Heavenly Courtesy.

Our Lady out of Nazareth rode –
It was Her month of heavy load;
Yet was Her face both great and kind,
For Courtesy was in Her Mind.

The third it was our Little Lord,
Whom all the Kings in arms adored;
He was so small you could not see
His large intent of Courtesy.

Our Lord, that was Our Lady's Son,
Go bless you, People, one by one;
My Rhyme is written, my work is done.

THE LEADER

The sword fell down: I heard a knell;
   I thought that ease was best,
And sullen men that buy and sell
   Were host: and I was guest.

All unashamed I sat with swine,
  We shook the dice for war,
The night was drunk with an evil wine –
  But she went on before.

  She rode a steed of the sea-foam breed,
    All faery was her blade,
  And the armour on her tender limbs
    Was of the moonshine made.

By God that sends the master-maids,
  I know not whence she came,
But the sword she bore to save the soul
  Went up like an altar flame
Where a broken race in a desert place
  Call on the Holy Name.

  We strained our eyes in the dim day-rise,
    We could not see them plain;
  But two dead men from Valmy fen
    Rode at her bridle-rein.

I hear them all, my fathers call,
  I see them how they ride,
And where had been that rout obscene
  Was an army straight with pride.
A hundred thousand marching men,
  Of squadrons twenty score,
And after them all the guns, the guns,
  But she went on before.

  Her face was like a king's command
    When all the swords are drawn.
  She stretched her arms and smiled at us
  Her head was higher than the hills.
  She led us to the endless plains.
    We lost her in the dawn.

A BIVOUAC

You came without a human sound,
    You came and brought my soul to me;
I only woke, and all around
They slumbered on the firelit ground,
    Beside the guns in Burgundy.

I felt the gesture of your hands,
    You signed my forehead with the Cross;
The gesture of your holy hands
Was bounteous – like the misty lands
    Along the Hills in Calvados.

But when I slept I saw your eyes,
    Hungry as death, and very far.
I saw demand in your dim eyes
Mysterious as the moons that rise
    At midnight, in the Pines of Var.

TO THE BALLIOL MEN STILL IN AFRICA

Years ago when I was at Balliol,
    Balliol men – and I was one –
Swam together in winter rivers,
    Wrestled together under the sun.
And still in the heart of us, Balliol, Balliol,
    Loved already, but hardly known,
Welded us each of us into the others:
    Called a levy and chose her own.

Here is a House that armours a man
    With the eyes of a boy and the heart of a ranger
And a laughing way in the teeth of the world
    And a holy hunger and thirst for danger:

[43]

Balliol made me, Balliol fed me,
   Whatever I had she gave me again:
And the best of Balliol loved and led me.
   God be with you, Balliol men.

I have said it before, and I say it again,
   There was treason done, and a false word spoken,
And England under the dregs of men,
   And bribes about, and a treaty broken:
But angry, lonely, hating it still,
   I wished to be there in spite of the wrong.
My heart was heavy for Cumnor Hill
   And the hammer of galloping all day long.

Galloping outward into the weather,
   Hands a-ready and battle in all:
Words together and wine together
   And song together in Balliol Hall.
Rare and single! Noble and few! . . .
   Oh! they have wasted you over the sea!
The only brothers ever I knew,
   The men that laughed and quarrelled with me.

                    .   .   .

Balliol made me, Balliol fed me,
   Whatever I had she gave me again;
And the best of Balliol loved and led me,
   God be with you, Balliol men.

THE REBEL

There is a wall of which the stones
Are lies and bribes and dead men's bones.
And wrongfully this evil wall
Denies what all men made for all,

And shamelessly this wall surrounds
Our homesteads and our native grounds.

But I will gather and I will ride,
And I will summon a countryside,
And many a man shall hear my halloa
Who never had thought the horn to follow;
And many a man shall ride with me
Who never had thought on earth to see
High Justice in her armoury.

When we find them where they stand,
A mile of men on either hand,
I mean to charge from right away
And force the flanks of their array,
And press them inward from the plains,
And drive them clamouring down the lanes,
And gallop and harry and have them down,
And carry the gates and hold the town.
Then shall I rest me from my ride
With my great anger satisfied.

Only, before I eat and drink,
When I have killed them all, I think
That I will batter their carven names,
And slit the pictures in their frames,
And burn for scent their cedar door,
And melt the gold their women wore,
And hack their horses at the knees,
And hew to death their timber trees,
And plough their gardens deep and through –
And all these things I mean to do
For fear perhaps my little son
Should break his hands, as I have done.

Strong God which made the topmost stars
  To circulate and keep their course,
Remember me; whom all the bars
  Of sense and dreadful fate enforce.

Above me in your heights and tall,
  Impassable the summits freeze,
Below the haunted waters call
  Impassable beyond the trees.

I hunger and I have no bread.
  My gourd is empty of the wine.
Surely the footsteps of the dead
  Are shuffling softly close to mine!

It darkens. I have lost the ford.
  There is a change on all things made.
The rocks have evil faces, Lord,
  And I am awfully afraid.

Remember me. The Voids of Hell
  Expand enormous all around.
Strong friend of souls, Emmanuel,
  Redeem me from accursed ground.

The long descent of wasted days,
  To these at last have led me down;
Remember that I filled with praise
The meaningless and doubtful ways
  That lead to an eternal town.

I challenged and I kept the Faith,
  The bleeding path alone I trod;
It darkens. Stand about my wraith,
  And harbour me, almighty God.

You wear the morning like your dress
And are with mastery crowned;
Whenas you walk your loveliness
Goes shining all around.
Upon your secret, smiling way
Such new contents were found,
The Dancing Loves made holiday
On that delighted ground.

Then summon April forth, and send
Commandment through the flowers;
About our woods your grace extend
A queen of careless hours.
For oh, not Vera veiled in rain,
Nor Dian's sacred Ring,
With all her royal nymphs in train,
Could so lead on the Spring.

THE RING

When I was flying before the King
In the wood of Valognes in my hiding,
Although I had not anything
I sent a woman a golden ring.

A Ring of the Moors beyond Leon
With emerald and with diamond stone,
And a writing no man ever had known,
And an opal standing all alone.

The shape of the ring the heart to bind:
The emerald turns from cold to kind:
The writing makes her sure to find: —
But the evil opal changed her mind.

Now when the King was dead, was he,
I came back hurriedly over the sea
From the long rocks in Normandy
To Bosham that is by Selsey.
And we clipt each other knee to knee.
But what I had was lost to me.

THE LITTLE SERVING MAID

There was a Queen of England,
  And a good Queen too.
She had a house in Powis Land
  With the Severn running through;
And Men-folk and Women-folk
  Apprenticed to a trade;
But the prettiest of all
  Was a Little Serving Maid.

'Oh Madam, Queen of England!
  Oh will you let me go!
For there's a Lad in London
  And he would have it so.
And I would have it too, Madam,
  And with him would I bide;
And he will be the Groom, Madam,
  And I shall be the Bride!'

'Oh fie to you and shame to you,
  You little Serving Maid!
And are you not astonied?
  And are you not afraid?
For never was it known
  Since Yngelonde began
That a Little Serving Maid
  Should go a-meeting of a man!'

Then the Little Serving Maid
   She went and laid her down,
With her cross and her beads,
   In her new courting gown.
And she called in Mother Mary's name
   And heavily she sighed:
'I think that I have come to shame!'
   And after that she died.

The good Queen of England
   Her women came and ran:
'The Little Serving Maid is dead
   From loving of a man!'
Said the good Queen of England
   'That is ill news to hear!
Take her out and shroud her,
   And lay her on a bier.'

They laid her on a bier,
   In the court-yard all;
Some came from Foresting,
   And some came from Hall.
And Great Lords carried her,
   And proud Priests prayed.
And that was the end
   Of the Little Serving Maid.

THE END OF THE ROAD

In these boots and with this staff
Two hundred leaguers and a half
Walked I, went I, paced I, tripped I,
Marched I, held I, skelped I, slipped I,
Pushed I, panted, swung and dashed I;
Picked I, forded, swam and splashed I,

Strolled I, climbed I, crawled and scrambled,
Dropped and dipped I, ranged and rambled;
Plodded I, hobbled I, trudged and tramped I,
And in lonely spinnies camped I,
And in haunted pinewoods slept I,
Lingered, loitered, limped and crept I,
Clambered, halted, stepped and leapt I;
Slowly sauntered, roundly strode I,
And . . .   (Oh, Patron saints and Angels
                That protect the four Evangels!
                And you Prophets vel majores
                Vel incerti, vel minores,
                Virgines ac confessores
                Chief of whose peculiar glories
                Est in Aula Regis stare
                Atque orare et exorare
                Et clamare et conclamare
                Clamantes cum clamoribus
                Pro Nobis Peccatoribus.)
Let me not conceal it . . . *Rode I.*
(For who but critics could complain
Of 'riding' in a railway train?)
Across the valleys and the high-land,
With all the world on either hand,
Drinking when I had a mind to,
Singing when I felt inclined to;
Nor ever turned my face to home
Till I had slaked my heart at Rome.

AN ORACLE THAT WARNED THE WRITER
WHEN ON PILGRIMAGE

Matutinus adest ubi Vesper, et accipiens te
Saepe recusatum voces intelligit hospes
Rusticus ignotas notas, ac flumina tellus
Occupat – In sancto tum, tum, stans Aede caveto
Tonsuram Hirsuti Capitis, via namque pedestrem
Ferrea praeveniens cursum, peregrine, laborem
Pro pietate tua inceptum frustratur, amore
Antiqui Ritus alto sub Numine Romae.

Translation of the above:

When early morning seems but eve
And they that still refuse receive:
When speech unknown men understand;
And floods are crossed upon dry land.
Within the Sacred Walls beware
The Shaven Head that boasts of Hair,
For when the road attains the rail
The Pilgrim's great attempt shall fail.

DRINKING SONG
ON THE EXCELLENCE OF BURGUNDY WINE

My jolly fat host with your face all a-grin,
Come, open the door to us, let us come in.
A score of stout fellows who think it no sin
If they toast till they're hoarse, and they drink till they spin,
    Hoofed it amain,
    Rain or no rain,
  To crack your old jokes, and your bottle to drain.

Such a warmth in the belly that nectar begets
As soon as his guts with its humour he wets,
The miser his gold, and the student his debts,
And the beggar his rags and his hunger forgets.
    For there's never a wine
    Like this tipple of thine
From the great hill of Nuits to the River of Rhine.

Outside you may hear the great gusts as they go
By Foy, by Duerne, and the hills of Lerraulx,
But the rain he may rain, and the wind he may blow,
If the Devil's above there's good liquor below.
    So it abound,
    Pass it around,
Burgundy's Burgundy all the year round.

DRINKING DIRGE

A thousand years ago I used to dine
    In houses where they gave me such regale
Of dear companionship and comrades fine
That out I went alone beyond the pale;
And riding, laughed and dared the skies malign
    To show me all the undiscovered tale –
But my philosophy's no more divine,
    I put my pleasure in a pint of ale.

And you, my friends, oh! pleasant friends of mine,
    Who leave me now alone, without avail,
On Californian hills you gave me wine,
    You gave me cider-drink in Longuevaile;
If after many years you come to pine
    For comradeship that is an ancient tale –
You'll find me drinking beer in Dead Man's Chine.
    I put my pleasure in a pint of ale.

In many a briny boat I've tried the brine,
  From many a hidden harbour I've set sail,
Steering towards the sunset where there shine
  The distant amethystine islands pale.
There are no ports beyond the far sea-line,
  Nor any halloa to meet the mariner's hail;
I stand at home and slip the anchor-line.
  I put my pleasure in a pint of ale.

Envoi

Prince! Is it true that when you go to dine
  You bring your bottle in a freezing pail?
Why then you cannot be a friend of mine.
  I put my pleasure in a pint of ale.

WEST SUSSEX DRINKING SONG

They sell good Beer at Haslemere
  And under Guildford Hill.
At Little Cowfold as I've been told
  A beggar may drink his fill:
There is a good brew in Amberley too,
  And by the bridge also;
But the swipes they take in at Washington Inn
  Is the very best Beer I know.

Chorus

With my here it goes, there it goes,
  All the fun's before us:
The Tipple's aboard and the night is young,
The door's ajar and the Barrel is sprung,
I am singing the best song ever was sung
  And it has a rousing chorus.

If I were what I never can be,
    The master or the squire:
If you gave me the hundred from here to the sea,
    Which is more than I desire:
Then all my crops should be barley and hops,
    And did my harvest fail
I'd sell every rood of mine acres I would
    For a belly-full of good Ale.

Chorus

With my here it goes, there it goes,
    All the fun's before us:
The Tipple's aboard and the night is young,
The door's ajar and the Barrel is sprung,
I am singing the best song ever was sung
    And it has a rousing Chorus.

A BALLAD ON SOCIOLOGICAL ECONOMICS

A while ago it came to pass
    (Merry we carol it all the day),
There sat a man on the top of an ass
    (Heart be happy and carol be gay
      In spite of the price of hay).

And over the down they hoofed it so
    (Happy go lucky has best of fare),
The man up above and the brute below
    (And singing we all forget to care
      A man may laugh if he dare).

Over the stubble and round the crop
    (Life is short and the world is round),
The donkey beneath and the man on the top
    (Oh! let good ale be found, be found,
      Merry good ale and sound).

[54]

It happened again as it happened before
   (Tobacco's a boon but ale is bliss),
The moke in the ditch and the man on the floor
   (And that is the moral to this, to this
     Remarkable artifice).

HERETICS ALL

Heretics all, whoever you be,
In Tarbes or Nimes, or over the sea,
You never shall have good words from me.
   Caritas non conturbat me.

But Catholic men that live upon wine
Are deep in the water, and frank, and fine;
Wherever I travel I find it so,
   Benedicamus Domino.

On childing women that are forlorn,
And men that sweat in nothing but scorn:
That is on all that ever were born,
   Miserere Domine.

To my poor self on my deathbed,
And all my dear companions dead,
Because of the love that I bore them,
   Dona Eis Requiem.

THE DEATH AND LAST CONFESSION
OF WANDERING PETER

When Peter Wanderwide was young
   He wandered everywhere he would:
And all that he approved was sung,
   And most of what he saw was good.

When Peter Wanderwide was thrown
   By Death himself beyond Auxerre,
He chanted in heroic tone
   To priests and people gathered there:

'If all that I have loved and seen
   Be with me on the Judgment Day,
I shall be saved the crowd between
   From Satan and his foul array.

'Almighty God will surely cry,
   "St Michael! Who is this that stands
With Ireland in his dubious eye,
   And Perigord between his hands,

' "And on his arm the stirrup-thongs,
   And in his gait the narrow seas,
And in his mouth Burgundian songs,
   But in his heart the Pyrenees?"

'St Michael then will answer right
   (And not without angelic shame),
"I seem to know his face by sight:
   I cannot recollect his name . . .?"

'St Peter will befriend me then,
   Because my name is Peter too:
'I know him for the best of men
   That ever wallopped barley brew.

"And though I did not know him well
   And though his soul were clogged with sin,
I hold the keys of Heaven and Hell.
   Be welcome, noble Peterkin."

[56]

'Then shall I spread my native wings
 And tread secure the heavenly floor,
And tell the Blessed doubtful things
 Of Val d'Aran and Perigord.'

.   .   .

This was the last and solemn jest
 Of weary Peter Wanderwide.
He spoke it with a failing zest,
 And having spoken it, he died.

DEDICATORY ODE

I mean to write with all my strength
 (It lately has been sadly waning)
A ballad of enormous length –
 Some parts of which will need explaining.[1]

Because (unlike the bulk of men
 Who write for fame or public ends)
I turn a lax and fluent pen
 To talking of my private friends.[2]

For no one, in our long decline,
 So dusty, spiteful and divided,
Had quite such pleasant friends as mine,
 Or loved them half as much as I did.

.   .   .

[1] But do not think I shall explain
 To any great extent. Believe me,
I partly write to give you pain,
 And if you do not like me, leave me.

[2] And least of all can you complain,
 Reviewers, whose unholy trade is,
To puff with all your might and main
 Biographies of single ladies.

[57]

The Freshman ambles down the High,
    In love with everything he sees,
He notes the racing autumn sky,
    He sniffs a lively autumn breeze.

'Can this be Oxford? This the place?'
    (He cries) 'of which my father said
The tutoring was a damned disgrace,
    The creed a mummery, stuffed and dead?

'Can it be here that Uncle Paul
    Was driven by excessive gloom
To drink and debt, and, last of all,
    To smoking opium in his room?

'Is it from here the people come,
    Who talk so loud, and roll their eyes,
And stammer? How extremely rum!
    How curious! What a great surprise!

'Some influence of a nobler day
    Than theirs (I mean than Uncle Paul's)
Has roused the sleep of their decay,
    And flecked with light their crumbling walls.

'O! dear undaunted boys of old,
    Would that your names were carven here,
For all the world in stamps of gold,
    That I might read them and revere.

'Who wrought and handed down for me
    This Oxford of the larger air,
Laughing, and full of faith, and free,
    With youth resplendent everywhere?'

Then learn: thou ill-instructed, blind,
  Young, callow, and untutored man,
Their private names were. . . .[1]
  Their club was called REPUBLICAN.

.   .   .

Where on their banks of light they lie,
  The happy hills of Heaven between,
The Gods that rule the morning sky
  Are not more young, nor more serene

Than were the intrepid Four that stand,
  The first who dared to live their dream.
And on this uncongenial land
  To found the Abbey of Theleme.

We kept the Rabelaisian plan:[2]
  We dignified the dainty cloisters
With Natural Law, the Rights of Man,
  Song, Stoicism, Wine and Oysters.

The library was most inviting:
  The books upon the crowded shelves
Were mainly of our private writing:
  We kept a school and taught ourselves.

We taught the art of writing things
  On men we still should like to throttle:
And where to get the Blood of Kings
  At only half a crown a bottle.

.   .   .

[1] Never mind.
[2] The plan forgot (I know not how,
    Perhaps the Refectory filled it),
  To put a chapel in; and now
    We're mortgaging the rest to build it.

Eheu Fugaces! Postume!
  (An old quotation out of mode);
My coat of dreams is stolen away
  My youth is passing down the road.

        .   .   .

The wealth of youth, we spent it well
  And decently, as very few can.
And is it lost? I cannot tell:
  And what is more, I doubt if you can.

The question's very much too wide,
  And much too deep, and much too hollow,
And learned men on either side
  Use arguments I cannot follow.

They say that in the unchanging place,
  Where all we loved is always dear,
We meet our morning face to face
  And find at last our twentieth year . . .

They say (and I am glad they say)
  It is so; and it may be so;
It may be just the other way,
  I cannot tell. But this I know:

From quiet homes and first beginning,
  Out to the undiscovered ends,
There's nothing worth the wear of winning,
  But laughter and the love of friends.

        .   .   .

But something dwindles, oh! my peers,
  And something cheats the heart and passes,
And Tom that meant to shake the years
  Has come to merely rattling glasses.

And He, the Father of the Flock,
   Is keeping Burmesans in order,
An exile on a lonely rock
   That overlooks the Chinese border.

And One (Myself I mean – no less),
   Ah! – will Posterity believe it –
Not only don't deserve success,
   But hasn't managed to achieve it.

Not even this peculiar town
   Has ever fixed a friendship firmer,
But – one is married, one's gone down,
   And one's a Don, and one's in Burmah.
      .   .   .

And oh! the days, the days, the days,
   When all the four were off together:
The infinite deep of summer haze,
   The roaring boast of autumn weather!
      .   .   .

I will not try the reach again,
   I will not set my sail alone,
To moor a boat bereft of men
   At Yarnton's tiny docks of stone.

But I will sit beside the fire,
   And put my hand before my eyes,
And trace, to fill my heart's desire,
   The last of all our Odysseys.

The quiet evening kept her tryst:
   Beneath an open sky we rode,
And passed into a wandering mist
   Along the perfect Evenlode.

The tender Evenlode that makes
    Her meadows hush to hear the sound
Of waters mingling in the brakes,
    And binds my heart to English ground.

A lovely river, all alone,
    She lingers in the hills and holds
A hundred little towns of stone,
    Forgotten in the western wolds.

.   .   .

I dare to think (though meaner powers
    Possess our thrones, and lesser wits
Are drinking worser wine than ours,
    In what's no longer Austerlitz)

That surely a tremendous ghost,
    The brazen-lunged, the bumper-filler,
Still sings to an immortal toast
    The Misadventures of the Miller.

The unending seas are hardly bar
    To men with such a prepossession:
We were? Why then, by God, we are –
    Order! I call the Club to session!

You do retain the song we set,
    And how it rises, trips and scans?
You keep the sacred memory yet,
    Republicans? Republicans?

You know the way the words were hurled,
    To break the worst of fortune's rub?
I give the toast across the world,
    And drink it, 'Gentlemen; the Club.'

When you and I were little boys
   We took a most impertinent delight
In foolish, painted and misshapen toys
   Which hidden mothers brought to us at night.

Do you that have the child's diviner part –
   The dear content a love familiar brings –
Take these imperfect toys, till in your heart
   They too attain the form of perfect things.

ON THE GIFT OF A BOOK TO A CHILD

Child! do not throw this book about!
   Refrain from the unholy pleasure
Of cutting all the pictures out!
   Preserve it as your chiefest treasure.

Child, have you never heard it said
   That you are heir to all the ages?
Why, then, your hands were never made
   To tear these beautiful thick pages!

Your little hands were made to take
   The better things and leave the worse ones:
They also may be used to shake
   The Massive Paws of Elder Persons.

And when your prayers complete the day,
   Darling, your little tiny hands
Were also made, I think, to pray
   For men that lose their fairylands.

[63]

And is it true? It is not true!
And if it was it wouldn't do
For people such as me and you,
Who very nearly all day long
Are doing something rather wrong.

HA'NACKER MILL

Sally is gone that was so kindly
    Sally is gone from Ha'nacker Hill.
And the Briar grows ever since then so blindly
    And ever since then the clapper is still,
    And the sweeps have fallen from Ha'nacker Mill.

H'anacker Hill is in Desolation:
    Ruin a-top and a field unploughed.
And Spirits that call on a fallen nation
    Spirits that loved her calling aloud:
    Spirits abroad in a windy cloud.

Spirits that call and no one answers;
    Ha'nacker's down and England's done.
Wind and Thistle for pipe and dancers
    And never a ploughman under the Sun.
    Never a ploughman. Never a one.

TARANTELLA

Do you remember an Inn,
Miranda?
Do you remember an Inn?

[64]

And the tedding and the spreading
Of the straw for a bedding,
And the fleas that tease in the High Pyrenees,
And the wine that tasted of the tar?
And the cheers and the jeers of the young muleteers
(Under the vine of the dark verandah)?
Do you remember an Inn, Miranda,
Do you remember an Inn?
And the cheers and the jeers of the young muleteers
Who hadn't got a penny,
And who weren't paying any,
And the hammer at the doors and the Din?
And the Hip! Hop! Hap!
Of the clap
Of the hands to the twirl and the swirl
Of the girl gone chancing,
Glancing,
Dancing,
Backing and advancing,
Snapping of a clapper to the spin
Out and in –
And the Ting, Tong, Tang of the Guitar!
Do you remember an Inn,
Miranda?
Do you remember an Inn!

Never more;
Miranda,
Never more.
Only the high peaks hoar:
And Aragon a torrent at the door.
No sound
In the walls of the Halls where falls

The tread
Of the feet of the dead to the ground
No sound:
But the boom
Of the far Waterfall like Doom.

THE CHAUNTY OF THE 'NONA'

Come list all ye Cullies and Doxies so dear,
You shall hearken to the tale of the Bold Marineer
That took ship out of Holyhead and drove her so hard
Past Bardsey, Pwllheli, Port Madoc, and Fishguard –
  Past Bardsey, Pwllheli, Port Madoc, and Fishguard.

Then he dropped out of Fishguard on a calm summer's day,
Past Strumbles, St David's and across St Bride's Bay;
Circumnavigating Skomer that island around,
With the heart of a Lion he threaded Jack Sound –
  With the heart of a Lion he threaded Jack Sound.

Then from out the Main Ocean there rolled a great cloud,
So he clawed into Milford Haven by the fog-blast so loud,
Until he dropped anchor in a deep-wooded bay,
Where all night with old Sleep and quiet Sadness he lay –
  Where all night with old Sleep and quiet Sadness he lay.

Next morning was a Doldrum, and he whistled for a breeze,
Which came from the Nor' Nor' Westward all across the high seas;
In passing St Govan's lightship he gave them good-night;
But before it was morning he raised Lundy Light –
  Before it was morning he had raised Lundy Light.

Then he tossed for twelve hours in that horrible place,
Which is known to the Mariner as the Great White Horse Race,
Till, with a slant about three bells, or maybe near four,
He saw white water breaking upon Loud Appledore –
  He saw white water breaking upon Loud Appledore.

The Pirates of Appledore, the Wines of Instow;
But her nose is for Bideford with the tide at the flow.
Rattle anchor, batten hatches, and falls all lie curled;
The Long Bridge of Bideford is the end of the World –
    The Long Bridge of Bideford is the end of the World.

THE WINGED HORSE

It's ten years ago today you turned me out o' doors
To cut my feet on flinty lands and stumble down the shores,
And I thought about the all-in-all, oh more than I can tell!
But I caught a horse to ride upon and I rode him very well,
He had flame behind the eyes of him and wings upon his side.
    And I ride, and I ride!

I rode him out of Wantage and I rode him up the hill,
And there I saw the Beacon in the morning standing still,
Inkpen and Hackpen and southward and away
High through the middle airs in the strengthening of the day,
And there I saw the channel-glint and England in her pride.
    And I ride, and I ride!

And once a-top of Lambourne down toward the hill of Clere
I saw the Host of Heaven in rank and Michael with his spear,
And Turpin out of Gascony and Charlemagne the Lord,
And Roland of the marches with his hand upon his sword
For the time he should have need of it, and forty more beside.
    And I ride, and I ride!

For you that took the all-in-all the things you left were three.
A loud voice for singing and keen eyes to see,
And a spouting well of joy within that never yet was dried!
    And I ride.

[67]

THE BALLAD OF VAL-ÈS-DUNES

THE VICTORY OF WILLIAM THE CONQUEROR IN HIS YOUTH OVER THE REBELS AT VAL-ÈS-DUNES IN THE YEAR 1047

I

The men that lived in Longuevaile
  Came out to fight by bands.
They jangled all in welded mail,
Their shields were rimmed of silver pale
And blazoned like a church-vitrail:
  Their swords were in their hands.
But the harsh raven of the Old Gods
  Was on the rank sea-sands.

.   .   .

There rose a wind on heath and den:
  The sky went racing grey.
The Bastard and his wall of men
  Were a charger's course away.

II

The Old Gods of the Northern Hall
  Are in their narrow room.
Their thrones are flanked of spearmen tall,
The three that have them in their thrall
Sit silently before them all,
  They weave upon their loom;
And round about them as they weave
  The Scalds sing doom.

III

The Bastard out of Normandy
  Was angry for his wrong.

His eyes were virginal to see,
For nothing in his heart had he
But a hunger for his great degree;
    And his back was broad and strong
As are the oxen of the field,
    That pull the ploughs along.

IV

He saw that column of cavalry wheel,
    Split outward, and deploy.
He heard, he heard the Oliphant peal.
He crooked an angry knee to feel
The scabbard against his gilded heel.
    He had great joy:
And he stood upright in the stirrup steel,
    Because he was a boy.

.   .   .

We faced their ordering, all the force,
    And there was little sound;
But Haribert-Le-Marshall's horse
    Pawed heavily the ground.

V

As the broad ships out of Barbary
    Come driving from the large,
With yards a-bend and courses free,
And tumbling down their decks a-lee
The hurrahing of the exultant sea,
    So drave they to the charge.
But the harsh raven of the Old Gods
    Was on the rank sea-marge.

VI

The old Gods of the Northern Hall
   Are crownéd for the tomb.
Their biers are flanked of torches tall,
And through the flames that leap and fall
There comes a droning and a call
   To the night's womb,
As the tide beneath a castle wall
   Goes drumming through the gloom.

VII

They tonsured me but Easter year,
   I swore to Christ and Rome.
My name is not mine older name . . .
But ah! to see them as they came,
With thundering and with points aflame,
   I smelt foam.
And my heart was like a wandering man's,
Who piles his boat on Moorna sands
   And serves a slave in alien lands,
And then beneath a harper's hands
   Hears suddenly of home.

    .   .   .

   For their cavalry came in a curling leaf,
    They shouted as they drave,
   And the Bastard's line was like a reef
    But theirs was like a wave.

VIII

As the broad ships out of Barbary
   Strike rock,
And the stem shatters, and the sail flaps;
Streaming seaward; and the taut shroud snaps,

And the block
    Clatters to the deck of the wreck,
So did the men of Longuevaile
    Take the shock.

IX

Our long line quivered but it did not break,
    It countered and was strong.
The first bolt went through the wind with a wail,
And another and a-many with a thudding on the mail;
Pattered all the arrows in an April hail;
    Whistled the ball and thong:
And I, the priest, with that began
    The singing of my song.

X

Press inward, inward, Normandy;
    Press inward, Cleres and Vaux;
Press inward, Mons and Valery;
    Press inward, Yvetot.
Stand hard the men of the Beechen Ford
(Oh! William of Falaise, my lord!)
Battle is a net and a struggle in a cord.
    Battle is a wrestler's throw.
The middle holding as the wings made good,
The far wings closing as the centre stood.
Battle is a mist and battle is a wood,
    And battle is won so.

XI

The fishermen fish in the River of Seine,
    They haul the long nets in.
They haul them in and they haul again,
(The fishermen fish in the River of Seine)

[71]

They haul them in and they haul again,
   A million glittering fin:
With the hauling in of our straining ends
   That Victory did begin.

XII

The tall son of the Seven Winds
   Galloped hot-foot from the Hither Hithe.
So strongly went he down the press,
Almost he did that day redress
With his holping and his hardiness,
   For his sword was like a scythe
In Arques when the grass is high,
And all the swaithes in order lie,
And there's the bailiff standing by –
   A-gathering of the tithe.

XIII

And now, go forward, Normandy,
   Go forward all in one.
The press was caught and trampled and it broke
From the sword and its swinger and the axe's stroke,
Pouring through the gap in a whirl of smoke
   As a blinded herd will run.
And so fled many and a very few
With mounts all spent would staggering pursue,
But the race fell scattered as the evening grew:
   The battle was over and done.

     .   .   .

Like birds against the reddening day
   They dwindled one by one,
And I heard a trumpet far away
   At the setting of the sun.

     .   .   .

XIV

The stars were in the Eternal Sky,
  It was calm in Massared;
Richard, Abbot of Leclair, and I
And a Picard Priest that held on high
  A Torch above his head;
We stumbled through the darkening land
Assoiling with anointed hand
  The dying and the dead.

XV

How many in the tufted grass,
  How many dead there lay.
For there was found the Fortenbras
And young Garain of Hault, alas!
And the Wardens of the Breton pass
  Who were lords of his array,
And Hugh that trusted in his glass
  But came not home the day.

XVI

I saw the miller of Martindall,
  I saw that archer die.
The blunt quarrel caught him at the low white wall,
And he tossed up his arrow to the Lord God of all,
But long before the first could fall
  His soul was in the sky.

XVII

The last of all the lords that sprang
  From Harcourt of the Crown,
He parried with the shield and the silver rang,
But the axe fell heavy on the helm with a clang

And the girths parted and the saddle swang,
    And he went down:
He never more sang winter songs
    In his high town.

XVIII

In his high town that Faëry is,
    And stands on Harcourt bay,
The fisher surging through the night
Takes bearing by that castle height,
And moors him harboured in the bight,
    And watches for the day.
But with the broadening of the light,
    It vanishes away.

XIX

In his high town that Faëry is,
    And stands on Harcourt Lea.
To summon him up his arrier-ban,
His writ beyond the mountains ran;
My father was his serving man,
    Although the farm was free.
Before the angry wars began
    He was a friend to me.

XX

The night before the boy was born
    There came a Priest who said
That he had seen red Aldeborn,
The star of hate in Taurus' horn,
Which glared above a field of corn,
    And covered him with dread.
I wish to God I had not held
    The cloth in which he bled.

            .   .   .

XXI

The Horse from Cleres and Valery,
    The foot from Yvetot,
And all the men of the Harbour Towns
    That live by fall and flow.
And all the men of the Beechen Ford
– Oh! William of Falaise, my lord! –
And all the sails in Michael's ward,
And all the shields of Caux,
    Shall follow you out across the world,
    With sword and lance and bow,
To Beachy and to Pevensey Bar,
    To Chester through the snow,
With sack and pack and camping tent,
    A-grumbling as they go:
My lord is William of Falaise.
    Haro!

This piece of verse is grossly unhistorical. Val-ès-Dunes is not on
the sea but inland. No Norman blazoned a shield or a church
window in the middle eleventh century, still less would he frame
one in silver, and I doubt gilt spurs. It was not the young Bastard
of Falaise, but the men of the King in Paris that really won the
battle. There was nothing Scandinavian left in Normandy, and
whatever there had been five generations before was slight. The
Cotentin had no more Scandinavian blood than the rest. There
is no such place as Longuevaile. There is a Hauteville, but it has
no bay and had nothing to do with the Harcourts, and the
Harcourts were not of blood-royal – and so forth.

TWELFTH NIGHT

As I was lifting over Down
A winter's night to Petworth Town,
I came upon a company
Of Travellers who would talk with me.

The riding moon was small and bright,
They cast no shadows in her light:
There was no man for miles a-near.
I would not walk with them for fear.

A star in heaven by Gumber glowed,
An ox across the darkness lowed,
Whereat a burning light there stood
Right in the heart of Gumber Wood.

Across the rime their marching rang,
And in a little while they sang;
They sang a song I used to know,
                    Gloria
In Excelsis Domino.

The frozen way those people trod
It led towards the Mother of God;
Perhaps if I had travelled with them
I might have come to Bethlehem.

THE SEASONS

They whom their mothers bare through Summer heat
Are boys of Autumn, and a fruit complete.

They whom their mothers bare through April rain
Are new as April, and as April vain.

They whom their mothers in dark Winters bare
Wake to a barren world, and straight despair.

But they that held through Winter to the Spring
Despair as I do, and, as I do, sing.

DOWN CHANNEL

The Channel pours out on the Ebb in a river gigantic.
   There is no Moon.
The Dark is low in a cloud on the huge Atlantic.
   We'll be raising the Lizard soon.

There will be no meeting of eyes, nor any blessing,
   After the run.
The lips are still and the hand has ceased from caressing.
   There is nothing more to be done.

THE CIGADAS

   Much louder was the Song of the Cigadas
      Upon the Mountain-side, before the day:
   The Mountain-side between the two Posadas,
      The two Posadas on Puerto Bay.
      I hear the Sussex Crickets in the hay.
   Much louder was the song of the Cigadas.

THE ISLANDS

Sing to me of the Islands, O daughter of Cohoolin, sing.
      Sing to me of the West:
Sing to me of the girth loosened and the lax harp string
      And of rest.

Beyond the skerries and beyond the outer water
      There lies the land.
Sing to me of the Islands, O daughter of Cohoolin, O High King's
      And of the Overstrand.   [daughter,

I desire to be with Brandan and his companions in the quiet places
      And to drink of their Spring.
Sing to me of the Islands and of the Blessed Faces,
      O Daughter of Cohoolin sing!

THE FIRE

We rode together all in pride,
They laughing in their riding gowns
We young men laughing at their side,
We charged at will across the downs.

We were companions. We were young.
We were immortal – so we said . . .
For that which in the heart was sung
Could have no commerce with the Dead.

Oh! We should live for ever! – Yes!
We were immortal – till there came
Command imposing loneliness
And an extinction of the flame.

And now it's over . . . How it rains!
And now it's over. Though the gale
Gives as of old its gallant hail,
A-driving at the window panes.

Lord! How the business disappears!
The golden faces charged with sense
Have broken to accept the years.
And look! what comes to Innocence!

The chosen pictures I retain
Shall perish quickly as shall I.
Only a little while remain
The Downs in their solemnity.

Were they not here, the girls and boys?
I hear them. They are at my call.
The stairs are full of ghostly noise,
But there is no one in the hall.

The firelight sinks: a reddening shade:
I watch alone beside the fire:
The fire of my good oak is made:
Where is the flower of my desire?

A canker caught it at the root:
A twisted stock: a barren Briar.
It withered. It will bear no fruit.
Where is the flower of my desire?

Absolve me, God, that in the land
Which I can nor regard nor know
Nor think about nor understand,
The flower of my desire shall blow.

                           *

In Barbary when I was young
   A woman singing through the night,
The scented lemon trees among
   In Barbary when I was young.

The song that in the night was sung,
   By Lailah the Rahabite.
In Barbary when I was young,
   A woman singing through the night.

FROM THE LATIN (BUT NOT SO PAGAN)

Blessed is he that has come to the heart of the world and is humble.
He shall stand alone; and beneath
His feet are implacable fate, and panic at night, and the strumble
Of the hungry river of death.

DISCOVERY

Life is a long discovery, isn't it?
You only get your wisdom bit by bit.
If you have luck you find in early youth
How dangerous it is to tell the Truth;
And next you learn how dignity and peace
Are the ripe fruits of patient avarice.
You find that middle life goes racing past.
You find despair: and, at the very last,
You find as you are giving up the ghost
That those who loved you best despised you most.

HEROIC POEM IN PRAISE OF WINE

TO DUFF COOPER

To exalt, enthrone, establish and defend,
To welcome home mankind's mysterious friend:
Wine, true begetter of all arts that be;
Wine, privilege of the completely free;
Wine the recorder; wine the sagely strong;
Wine, bright avenger of sly-dealing wrong,
Awake, Ausonian Muse, and sing the vineyard song!

Sing how the Charioteer from Asia came,
And on his front the little dancing flame
Which marked the God-head. Sing the Panther-team,
The gilded Thyrsus twirling, and the gleam
Of cymbals through the darkness. Sing the drums.
He comes: the young renewer of Hellas comes!
The Seas await him. Those Aegean Seas
Roll from the dawning, ponderous, ill at ease,
In lifts of lead, whose cresting hardly breaks

To ghostly foam, when suddenly there awakes
A mountain glory inland. All the skies
Are luminous; and amid the sea bird cries
The mariner hears a morning breeze arise.
Then goes the Pageant forward. The sea-way
Silvers the feet of that august array
Trailing above the waters, through the airs;
And as they pass a wind before them bears
The quickening word, the influence magical.
The Islands have received it, marble-tall;
The long shores of the mainland. Something fills
The warm Euboean combes, the sacred hills
Of Aulis and of Argos. Still they move
Touching the City walls, the Temple grove,
Till, far upon the horizon-glint, a gleam
Of light, of trembling light, revealed they seem
Turned to a cloud, but to a cloud that shines,
And everywhere as they pass, the Vines! The Vines!
The Vines, the conquering Vines! And the Vine breathes
Her savour through the upland, empty heaths
Of treeless wastes; the Vines have come to where
The dark Pelasgian steep defends the lair
Of the wolf's hiding; to the empty fields
By Aufidus, the dry campaign that yields
No harvest for the husbandman, but now
Shall bear a nobler foison than the plough;
To where, festooned along the tall elm trees,
Tendrils are mirrored in Tyrrhenian seas;
To where the South awaits them; even to where
Stark, African, informed of burning air,
Upturned to Heaven the broad Hipponian plain
Extends luxurious and invites the main.
Guelma's a mother: barren Thapsa breeds;
And northward in the valleys, next the meads
That sleep by misty river banks, the Vines

Have struck to spread below the solemn pines.
The Vines are on the roof-trees. All the Shrines
And Homes of men are consecrate with Vines.

And now the task of that triumphant day
Has reached to victory. In the reddening ray
With all his train, from hard Iberian lands
Fulfilled, apparent, that Creator stands
Halted on Atlas. Far beneath him, far,
The strength of Ocean darkening and the star
Beyond all shores. There is a silence made.
It glorifies: and the gigantic shade
Of Hercules adores him from the West.
Dead Lucre: burnt Ambition: Wine is best.

But what are these that from the outer murk
Of dense mephitic vapours creeping lurk
To breathe foul airs from that corrupted well
Which oozes slime along the floor of Hell?
These are the stricken palsied brood of sin
In whose vile veins, poor, poisonous and thin,
Decoctions of embittered hatreds crawl:
These are the Water-Drinkers, cursed all!
On what gin-sodden Hags, what flaccid sires
Bred these White Slugs from what exhaust desires?
In what close prison's horror were their wiles
Watched by what tyrant power with evil smiles;
Or in what caverns, blocked from grace and air
Received they, then, the mandates of despair?
What! Must our race, our tragic race, that roam
All exiled from our first, and final, home: tost
That in one moment of temptation lost
Our heritage, and now wander, hunger-
Beyond the Gates (still speaking with our eyes

[82]

For ever of remembered Paradise),
Must we with every gift accepted, still,
With every joy, receive attendant ill?
Must some lewd evil follow all our good
And muttering dog our brief beatitude?

A primal doom, inexorable, wise,
Permitted, ordered, even these to rise.
Even in the shadow of so bright a Lord
Must swarm and propagate the filthy horde
Debased, accursed I say, abhorrent and abhorred.
Accursed and curse-bestowing. For whosoe'er
Shall suffer their contagion, everywhere
Falls from the estate of man and finds his end
To the mere beverage of the beast condemned.
For such as these in vain the Rhine has rolled
Imperial centuries by hills of gold;
For such as these the flashing Rhone shall rage
In vain its lightning through the Hermitage,
Or level-browed divine Touraine receive
The tribute of her vintages at eve.
For such as these Burgundian heats in vain
Swell the rich slope or load the empurpled plain.
Bootless for such as these the mighty task
Of bottling God the Father in a flask
And leading all Creation down distilled
To one small ardent sphere immensely filled.
With memories empty, with experience null,
With vapid eye-balls meaningless and dull
They pass unblest through the unfruitful light;
And when we open the bronze doors of Night,
When we in high carousal, we, reclined,
Spur up to Heaven the still ascending mind,
Pass with the all inspiring, to and fro,
The torch of genius and the Muse's glow,

They, lifeless, stare at vacancy alone
Or plan mean traffic, or repeat their moan.
We, when repose demands us, welcomed are
In young white arms, like our great Exemplar
Who, wearied with creation, takes his rest
And sinks to sleep on Ariadne's breast.
They through the darkness into darkness press
Despised, abandoned and companionless.
And when the course of either's sleep has run
We leap to life like heralds of the sun;
We from the couch in roseate mornings gay
Salute as equals the exultant day
While they, the unworthy, unrewarded, they
The dank despisers of the Vine, arise
To watch grey dawns and mourn indifferent skies.

Forget them! Form the Dionysian ring
And pulse the ground, and Io, Io, sing.

Father Lenæan, to whom our strength belongs,
Our lives, our wars, our laughter and our songs,
Remember our inheritance, who praise
Your glory in these last unhappy days
When beauty sickens and a muddied robe
Of baseness fouls the universal globe.
Though all the Gods indignant and their train
Abandon ruined man, do thou remain!
By thee the vesture of our life was made,
The Embattled Gate, the lordly Colonnade,
The woven fabric's gracious hues, the sound
Of trumpets, and the quivering fountain-round,
And, indestructible, the Arch, and, high,
The Shaft of Stone that stands against the sky,
And, last, the guardian-genius of them, Rhyme,

Come from beyond the world to conquer time:
All these are thine, Lenæan.

By thee do seers the inward light discern;
By thee the statue lives, the Gods return;
By thee the thunder and the falling foam
Of loud Acquoria's torrent call to Rome;
Alba rejoices in a thousand springs,
Gensano laughs, and Orvieto sings . . .
But, Ah! With Orvieto, with that name
Of dark Etrurian, subterranean flame
The years dissolve. I am standing in that hour
Of majesty Septembral, and the power
Which swells the clusters when the nights are still
With autumn stars on Orvieto hill.

Had these been mine, Ausonian Muse, to know
The large contented oxen heaving slow;
To count my sheaves at harvest; so to spend
Perfected days in peace until the end;
With every evening's dust of gold to hear
The bells upon the pasture height, the clear
Full horn of herdsmen gathering in the kine
To ancient byres in hamlets Apennine,
And crown abundant age with generous ease:
Had these, Ausonian Muse, had these, had these . . .

But since I would not, since I could not stay,
Let me remember even in this my day
How, when the ephemeral vision's lure is past,
All, all, must face their Passion at the last . . .
Was there not one that did to Heaven complain
How, driving through the midnight and the rain,
He struck, the Atlantic seethe and surge before,

Wrecked in the North along a lonely shore
To make the lights of home and hear his name no more.
Was there not one that from a desperate field
Rode with no guerdon but a rifted shield;
A name disherited; a broken sword;
Wounds unrenowned; battle beneath no Lord;
Strong blows, but on the void, and toil without reward.

When from the waste of such long labour done
I too must leave the grape-ennobling sun
And like the vineyard worker take my way
Down the long shadows of declining day,
Bend on the sombre plain my clouded sight
And leave the mountain to the advancing night,
Come to the term of all that was mine own
With nothingness before me, and alone;
Then to what hope of answer shall I turn?
Comrade-Commander whom I dared not earn,
What said You then to trembling friends and few?
'A moment, and I drink it with you new:
But in my Father's Kingdom.' So, my Friend,
Let not Your cup desert me in the end.
But when the hour of mine adventure's near,
Just and benignant let my youth appear
Bearing a Chalice, open, golden, wide,
With benediction graven on its side.
So touch my dying lip: so bridge that deep:
So pledge my waking from the gift of sleep,
And, sacramental, raise me the Divine:
Strong brother in God and last companion, Wine.

Lo! Very far away, like evening bells
At the sun's setting, from the darkening years
Come love, and love's old purity, and tears,
And man to man strong-faced; such thought as wells
From earth's first life; I hear the din of lying,
I hear strange sounds, and tumult, and the hell
Of hydra-headed mob that barks its knell,
Through which the music of thy song undying
O only glory! is as sweet and clear
As when first heard in some old fire-lit hall,
From the strong harp it called the memory dear
Of deed, and death, and fiery trumpet-call,
And told the story of the laughing tear;
When strongly warring with thy trembling lips,
Old to the old, thou brought'st the far times near;
And sang'st the battle round the hollow ships,
The while Odysseus bent his hoary head to hear.

★

As one who hath sent forth on a bold emprise
Into some distant land his Argosies
Watches in dread the fitful changing breeze,
And as now soft, now rude, its voices rise,
So hopes, so fears, for his far merchandise,
(Though that in other climes have other seas),
I, anxious too that this my plea should please,
Gaze still upon the mystery of your eyes;
The which, now laughing, now provoking sorrow,
Most like a fitful breeze have seemed to me;

But roofy night can breed an open morrow,
And these rough winds give earnest presently
Of days when, heeling down the waves, shall come
All my dear fleet and all my risked adventures Home.

EHEU! FUGACES

Two years ago, or it may be three,
Lord! how time passes,
Especially with me!
Eheu fugaces!
May we not play in the woods again,
Lads to the lasses!
Must we be men?
Eheu fugaces!
Still blows the wind and the rain comes down
All the window glasses
Of this dirty town.
Eheu fugaces!

SONG IN THE OLD MANNER

C'est ma Jeunesse qui s'en va.
Adieu! la très gente compagne –
Oncques ne suis moins gai pour ça
(C'est ma Jeunesse qui s'en va)
Et lon-lon-laire, et lon-lon-là
Peut-être perds; peut-être gagne.
C'est ma Jeunesse qui s'en va.

[The twelve poems following are part of the text of 'The Four Men']

THE SOUTHERN HILLS AND THE SOUTH SEA

The Southern Hills and the South Sea
They blow such gladness into me,
That when I get to Burton Sands
And smell the smell of the Home Lands,
My heart is all renewed and fills
With the Southern Sea and the South Hills.

THE FIRST DRINKING SONG

On Sussex hills where I was bred,
When lanes in autumn rains are red,
When Arun tumbles in his bed,
    And busy great gusts go by;
When branch is bare in Burton Glen
And Bury Hill is a-whitening, then,
I drink strong ale with gentlemen;
        Which nobody can deny, deny,
          Deny, deny, deny, deny,
            Which nobody can deny!

In half-November off I go,
To push my face against the snow,
And watch the winds wherever they blow,
    Because my heart is high:
Till I settle me down in Steyning to sing
Of the women I met in my wandering,
And of all that I mean to do in the spring.
        Which nobody can deny, deny,
          Deny, deny, deny, deny,
            Which nobody can deny!

Then times be rude and weather be rough,
And ways be foul and fortune tough,
We are of the stout South Country stuff,
That never can have good ale enough,
    And do this chorus cry!
From Crowboro' Top to Ditchling Down,
From Hurstpierpoint to Arundel town,
The girls are plump and the ale is brown:
    Which nobody can deny, deny,
      Deny, deny, deny, deny!
      If he does he tells a lie!

SONG OF THE PELAGIAN HERESY FOR THE STRENGTHENING
OF MEN'S BACKS AND THE VERY ROBUST OUT-THRUSTING
OF DOUBTFUL DOCTRINE AND THE UNCERTAIN
INTELLECTUAL

Pelagius lived in Kardanoel,
    And taught a doctrine there,
How whether you went to Heaven or Hell,
    It was your own affair.
How, whether you found eternal joy
    Or sank forever to burn,
It had nothing to do with the Church, my boy,
    But was your own concern.

Semi-chorus

Oh, he didn't believe
In Adam and Eve,
    He put no faith therein!
His doubts began
With the fall of man,
    And he laughed at original sin!

[90]

With my row-ti-tow, ti-oodly-ow,
   He laughed at original sin!

Whereat the Bishop of old Auxerre
   (Germanus was his name),
He tore great handfuls out of his hair,
   And he called Pelagius Shame:
And then with his stout Episcopal staff
   So thoroughly thwacked and banged
The heretics all, both short and tall,
   They rather had been hanged.

Semi-chorus

Oh, he thwacked them hard, and he banged them long,
   Upon each and all occasions,
Till they bellowed in chorus, loud and strong,
   Their orthodox persuasions!

Chorus

With my row-ti-tow, ti-oodly-ow,
   Their orthodox persu-a-a-sions!

Now the Faith is old and the Devil is bold,
   Exceedingly bold indeed;
And the masses of doubt that are floating about
   Would smother a mortal creed.
But we that sit in a sturdy youth,
   And still can drink strong ale,
Oh – let us put it away to infallible truth,
   Which always shall prevail!

Semi-chorus
And thank the Lord
For the temporal sword,
   And howling heretics too;
And whatever good things
Our Christendom brings,
   But especially barley brew!

Chorus
With my row-ti-tow, ti-oodly-ow,
   Especially barley brew!

THE SONG CALLED
'HIS HIDE IS COVERED WITH HAIR'

The dog is a faithful, intelligent friend,
   But his hide is covered with hair;
The cat will inhabit the house to the end,
   But *her* hide is covered with hair.

The hide of the mammoth was covered with wool,
The hide of the porpoise is sleek and cool,
But you'll find, if you look at that gambolling fool,
   That his hide is covered with hair.

Oh, I thank my God for this at the least,
I was born in the West and not in the East,
And He made me a human instead of a beast,
   Whose hide is covered with hair!

The cow in the pasture that chews the cud,
   Her hide is covered with hair.
And even a horse of the Barbary blood,
   His hide is covered with hair!

[92]

The camel excels in a number of ways,
And travellers give him unlimited praise –
He can go without drinking for several days –
  But his hide is covered with hair.

The bear of the forest that lives in a pit,
  His hide is covered with hair;
The laughing hyena in spite of his wit,
  His hide is covered with hair!

The Barbary ape and the chimpanzee,
And the lion of Africa, verily he,
With his head like a wig, and the tuft on his knee,
  His hide . . .

A THRENODY FOR THE DEPARTING YEAR

['Grizzlebeard: "Is there a tune?"
The Poet: "There is a sort of dirge." ']

Attend, my gentle brethren of the Weald,
Whom now the frozen field
Does with his caking shell your labour spurn,
And turn your shares and turn
Your cattle homeward to their lazy byres;
Oh! gather round our fires
And point a stave or scald a cleanly churn
The while
With ritual strict and nice observance near,
We weave in decent rhyme
A Threnody for the Departing Year.

And you that since the weary world began,
Subject and dear to man,
Have made a living noise about our homes,
You cows and geese and pigs and sheep and all the crew

Of mice and coneys too
And hares and all that ever lurks and roams
From Harting all the way to Bodiam bend,
Attend!
It is a solemn time,
And we assembled here
Advance in honourable rhyme
With ritual strict and nice observance near
Our Threnody for the Departing Year.

The year shall pass, and yet again the year
Shall on our reeds return
The tufted reeds to hurrying Arun dear . . .

As I was passing up your landing towns
I heard how in the South a goddess lay . . .

She ends our little cycle with a pall:
The winter snow shall reverently fall
On our beloved lands
As on Marana dead a winding sheet
Was laid to hide the smallness of her hands,
And her lips virginal:
Her virginal white feet.

HIS OWN COUNTRY

I shall go without companions,
    And with nothing in my hand;
I shall pass through many places
    That I cannot understand –
Until I come to my own country,
    Which is a pleasant land!

The trees that grow in my own country
   Are the beech tree and the yew;
Many stand together,
   And some stand few.
In the month of May in my own country
   All the woods are new.

When I get to my own country
   I shall lie down and sleep;
I shall watch in the valleys
   The long flocks of sheep.
And then I shall dream, for ever and all,
   A good dream and deep.

THE SAILOR'S CAROL

Noël! Noël! Noël! Noël!
A Catholic tale have I to tell!
And a Christian song have I to sing
While all the bells in Arundel ring.

I pray good beef and I pray good beer
This holy night of all the year,
But I pray detestable drink for them
That give no honour to Bethlehem.

May all good fellows that here agree
Drink Audit Ale in heaven with me,
And may all my enemies go to hell!
Noël! Noël! Noël! Noël!
May all my enemies go to hell!
Noël! Noël!

Duke William was a wench's son,
    His grandfer was a tanner!
He drank his cider from the tun,
    Which is the Norman manner:
His throne was made of oak and gold,
    His bow-shaft of the yew –
That is the way the tale is told,
    I doubt if it be true!

    But what care I for him?
    My tankard is full to the brim,
    And I'll sing Elizabeth, Dorothy,
        Margaret, Mary, Dorinda, Persephone, Miriam,
    Pegotty taut and trim.

The men that sailed to Normandy
    Foul weather may they find;
For banging about in the waist of a ship
    Was never to my mind.
They drink their rum in the glory-hole
    In quaking and in fear;
But a better man was left behind,
    And he sits drinking beer.

    But what care I for the swine?
    They never were fellows of mine!
    And I'll sing Elizabeth, Dorothy,
        Margaret, Mary, Dorinda,
        Persephone, Miriam, Pegotty,
        Jezebel, Topsy, Andromeda,
        Magdalen, Emily, Charity, Agatha, Beatrice,
        Anna, Cecilia, Maud, Cleopatra, Selene,
        and Jessica . . .
                    Barbara stout and fine.

I am sailing for America
That far foreign strand,
And I whopes to set foot
In a fair fruitful land,
But in the midst of the ocean
May grow the green apple tree
Avoor I prove faalse
To the girl that loves me.

The moon shall be in darkness,
And the stars give no light
But I'll roll you in my arms
On a cold frosty night.
And in the midst of the ocean
May grow the green apple tree
Avoor I prove faalse
To the girl that loves me.

ON THE SPIRIT OF GETTING-ON-ED-NESS

['The Sailor: "She whom we rail at in this song is that Spirit
of getting-on-ed-ness and making out our life at the expense
of our fellow men and of our own souls." ']

Thou ugly, lowering, treacherous Quean
    I think thou art the Devil!
To pull them down the rich and mean,
    And bring them to one level.
        Of all my friends
        That found their ends
By only following thee,
        How many I tell
        Already in Hell,
So shall it not be with me!

I knew three fellows were in your thrall,
  Got more than they could carry,
The first might drink no wine at all,
  And the second he would not marry;
The third in seeking golden earth
  Was drownded in the sea,
Which taught him what your wage is worth,
  So shall it not be with me!

There was Peter Bell of North Chappel,
  Was over hard and sparing,
He spent no penny of all his many,
  And died of over caring;
He saved above two underd pound
  But his widow spent it free,
And turned the town nigh upside down,
  So shall it not be with me!

Then mannikins bang the table round,
  For the younger son o' the Squire,
Who never was blest of penny or pound,
  But got his heart's desire.
Oh, the Creditors' curse
  Might follow his hearse,
For all that it mattered to he!
  They were easy to gammon
  From worshipping Mammon,
So shall it not be with me!

  And Absalom,
  That was a King's son,
Was hangéd on a tree,
  When he the Kingdom would have won,
So shall it not be with me!

'So I put down in fragments this line and that.'

and therefore even youth that dies
May leave of right its legacies.

and of mine opulence I leave
To every Sussex girl and boy
My lot in universal joy.

One with our random fields we grow.

because of lineage and because
The soil and memories out of mind
Embranch and broaden all mankind.

And I shall pass, but this shall stand
Almost as long as No-Man's Land.

★

[' "No, certainly", I answered to myself aloud, "he does not die!"
Then from that phrase there ran the fugue . . .']

He does not die that can bequeath
Some influence to the land he knows,
Or dares, persistent, interwreath
Love permanent with the wild hedgerows;
    He does not die, but still remains
    Substantiate with his darling plains.

The spring's superb adventure calls
His dust athwart the woods to flame;
His boundary river's secret falls
Perpetuate and repeat his name,
    He rides his loud October sky:
    He does not die. He does not die.

[99]

The beeches know the accustomed head
Which loved them, and a peopled air
Beneath their benediction spread
Comforts the silence everywhere;
    For native ghosts return and these
    Perfect the mystery in the trees.

So, therefore, though myself be crosst
The shuddering of that dreadful day
When friend and fire and home are lost
And even children drawn away –
    The passer-by shall hear me still,
    A boy that sings on Duncton Hill.

★

['It would seem to be like man's attempt to resist time in the case
of his own body, of which the poet has written . . .']

There is no fortress of man's flesh so made
But subtle, treacherous Time comes creeping in.
Oh, long before his last assaults begin
The enemy's on; the stronghold is betrayed;
And the one lonely watchman, half-dismayed,
Beyond the covering dark, he hears them come:
The distant hosts of Death that march with muffled drum.

TO THE 8TH REGIMENT OF ARTILLERY
IN THE FRENCH SERVICE
now in Garrison at Nancy. P.P.C.

Freedom is up for sale and all assess her;
The Tyrants have put in their ancient pleas;
The Usurers are the heirs of the Oppressor;
The insolent boast of Hell is on the High Seas.

The Sword that was the strength of the poor is broken;
The wrath that was the wealth of the poor is spent;
Witless are all the great words we have spoken –
But you, my regiment?

You that put down the mighty from their seat,
And fought to fill the hungry with good things,
And turned the rich men empty to the street,
And trailed your scabbards in the halls of Kings.

Do you remember how you cleared the timber
At Leipzig, holding an unequal fight,
Or heard Ney shouting for the guns to unlimber,
And hold the Beresina Bridge at night?

Do you remember the immortal chorus,
In Valmy fog, and where our Captains stood
Till the cannonade had opened the world before us
To the broad daylight and the pride of the Latin blood?

The Sword that was the strength of the poor is broken;
The wrath that was the wealth of the poor is spent;
Witless are all the great words we have spoken –
But you, my regiment?

THE POET SINGS OF THE NORTH SEA

The moving mind that God gave me
Is manifold as the wide North Sea,
And as the sea is full of things,
The great fish in their wanderings
And the spread galleys of the old kings
And darkness eddying round in rings,
So, packed with all that I have done
And felt and known and lost and won,
By the tide drifted and the wind inclined
Moves my not measurable mind.

DESERT

I stood in the desert, and I watched the snows
On Aures, in their splendour from the west.
Sahara darkened: and I thought of those
That hold in isolation and are blest.

They that in dereliction grow perfected:
They that are silent: they that stand apart:
They that shall judge the world as God's elected:
They that have had the sword athwart the heart.

TRIOLET

The young, the lovely and the wise
    Their face is set toward their going.
They pass me with indifferent eyes,
The young, the lovely and the wise,
And fill me with a long surmise
Upon my losing and my owing . . .
The young, the lovely and the wise
    Their face is set toward their going.

DECAMERON

Maia, Ridalvo, Brangwen, Amoreth,
In mountain-guarded gardens vainly gay,
Wasted the irrecoverable breath,
And sought to lose in play
The fixed, majestic, questioning eyes of Death
By turning theirs away.

I love to roam from mere caprice
From town to town, from time to time,
Accompanied by Mrs Rhys,
And singing her an elfin rhyme:
  'Star of my wanderings Mrs Rhys,
  When Mr Rhys shall hear that we
  Were going on like little geese,
  It will annoy him damnably.'

And when because we lack the tin
To pay the sums which they require,
McKenna's minions run us in,
I'll warble in the Black Maria:
  'Light of my dungeon Mrs Rhys,
When Mr Rhys shall come to find
That you are pinched to stretch a piece,
The thing will prey upon his mind.
End of existence Mrs Rhys,
  When Mr Rhys shall hear that you
Are in the hands of the police
It will disturb him not a few.'

TO JULIET'S GUARDIAN ANGEL

You that now some thirty odd
Years ago were set by God,
Years ago the task were set,
Of protecting Juliet –
Keep her sleeping, keep her waking,
Keep her giving, keep her taking,
Keep her safe among the tricks
Of surrounding Heretics;

[103]

Keep her always, right or wrong,
Keep her weak, and keep her strong,
Keep her young about the eyes,
And lead her on to Paradise.

JULIET

How did the party go in Portman Square?
I cannot tell you; Juliet was not there.
And how did Lady Gaster's party go?
Juliet was next me and I do not know.

★

When Juliet sleeps, the whispering watcher sings
Her lids the loveliest of all lovely things –
But when she wakes, he knows in glad surprise
Those lovely lids less lovely than those eyes.

★

Are there Muses? are there Graces?
Are there then immortal faces?
No man mortal saw them yet.
I today saw Juliet.

★

Two visions permanent: his native place
Found after days at sea, and Juliet's face.

★

Some say that Juliet found a Friend, and some
Say that the Friend she found was far too dumb;
And some say Juliet never found him: no;
But he found Juliet: Gloria Domino.

First in his pride the orient sun's display
Renews the world, and changes night to day.
A little later – round about eleven –
Juliet appears, and changes earth to heaven.

★

Goodbye my Juliet; may you always be
Polite to all the world but kind to me.

★

The little owl that Juliet loved is dead:
Pallas Athene took him, when she said
She brooked no rival: meaning by this word
That Aphrodite should not keep her bird.

★

Three Graces, Muses nine, of Pleiads seven,
But Juliet one, beneath an empty Heaven.

★

Verse should be set to Music. This is set
To Music: and the Music's Juliet.

ROSE

Rose, little Rose, the youngest of the Roses,
My little Rose whom I may never see,
When you shall come to where the heart reposes
Cut me a Rose and send it down to me.

When you shall come into the High Rose-Gardens,
Where Roses bend upon Our Lady's Tree,
The place of Plenitudes, the place of Pardons,
Cut me a Rose and send it down to me.

ON THE FLY LEAF OF AN EDITION OF
THE WORKS OF RABELAIS:

To Philip Comyns Carr
As also these lovely verses
Dec. 7 1898

Lord, I hear the people say
That on thy awful judgement day
I most certainly shall stand
With the rest on thy left hand.
Lord, observe my little prayer;
When the good men see me there
And the noisy anthem floats
From the Non-conformist throats,
Give me, Lord, a place apart.
Laughter kept me clean of heart.

EPITAPH

Ci gît celui qui t'aimais trop
Pour ton bonheur et son repos.

ON HER PICTURE

It isn't like you: So? I'm glad to say
There's nothing like you upon earth today.

ON THE STAIR

Here I saw my Juliet pass
And a glory in the glass.
Glass how can you bear it, how,
To mirror other faces now?

[106]

*

Does Juliet change her room? I hate the change
Which turns the setting of that diamond strange!
Yet should I grateful be for change that proves
Unchangeable my honours and my loves.

FAREWELL TO JULIET

How shall I round the ending of a story,
    Now the wind's falling and the harbour nears?
How shall I sign your tiny Book of Glory,
    Juliet, my Juliet, after many years?

I'll sign it, One that halted at a vision:
    One whom the shaft of beauty struck to flame:
One that so wavered in a strong decision:
    One that was born perhaps to fix your name.

One that was pledged, and goes to his replevining:
    One that now leaves you with averted face,
A shadow passing through the doors at evening
    To his companion and his resting place.

EPIGRAMS

ON PERKINS: AN ACTOR

Perkins' Duchesses have marked a great
Improvement in his coster scene of late.
He gives the oath, the drunken lurch, the roar,
As even Perkins never did before.
And yet, the model is not far to seek –
Perkins was visiting at home last week.

ON SLOP: A POET

Where Mr Slop particularly shines
Is in his six sonorous single lines.
Perhaps where he is less successful is
In all the other verses. These are his.

ON TORTURE: A PUBLIC SINGER

Torture will give a dozen pence or more
To keep a drab from bawling at his door.
The public taste is quite a different thing –
Torture is positively paid to sing.

ON SUBTLE: A REVIEWER

Subtle – your keen analysis and nice,
Like everything about you, has its price.
When you express your owner's private spite
A Pound rewards the virulence you write.
A Pound should therefore buy your praise; well, then,
Why should the Author have to pay you ten?

ON PAUNCH: A PARASITE

Paunch talks against good liquor to excess,
And then about his raving Patroness;
And then he talks about himself. And then
We turn the conversation on to men.

ON PUGLEY: A DON
Pugley denies the soul? Why, so do I
The soul, of Pugley, heartily deny.

THE MIRROR
The mirror held your fair, my Fair,
A fickle moment's space.
You looked into mine eyes, and there
For ever fixed your face.

Keep rather to your looking-glass
Than my more constant eyes:
It told the truth – Alas! my lass,
My faithful memory lies.

ON HYGIENE
Of old when folk lay sick and sorely tried
The doctors gave them physic, and they died.
But here's a happier age: for now we know
Both how to make men sick and keep them so.

THE FALSE HEART
I said to Heart, 'How goes it?' Heart replied:
'Right as a Ribstone Pippin!' But it lied.

ON BENICIA: WHO WISHED HIM WELL
Benicia wished me well; I wished her well.
And what I wished her more I may not tell.

ON HIS BOOKS
When I am dead, I hope it may be said:
'His sins were scarlet, but his books were read.'

ON NOMAN: A GUEST
Dear Mr Noman, does it ever strike you,
The more we see of you, the less we like you?

A TRINITY

Of three in One and One in three
My narrow mind would doubting be
Till Beauty, Grace and Kindness met
And all at once were Juliet.

ON LADY POLTAGRUE: A PUBLIC PERIL

The Devil, having nothing else to do,
Went off to tempt My Lady Poltagrue.
My Lady, tempted by a private whim,
To his extreme annoyance, tempted him.

THE ELM

This is the place where Dorothea smiled.
I did not know the reason, nor did she.
But there she stood, and turned, and smiled at me:
A sudden glory had bewitched the child.
The corn at harvest, and a single tree.
This is the place where Dorothea smiled.

THE TELEPHONE

To-night in million-voicèd London I
Was lonely as the million-pointed sky
Until your single voice. Ah! So the sun
Peoples all heaven, although he be but one.

THE STATUE

When we are dead, some Hunting-boy will pass
And find a stone half-hidden in tall grass
And grey with age: but having seen that stone
(Which was your image), ride more slowly on.

EPITAPH ON THE FAVOURITE DOG
OF A POLITICIAN

Here lies a Dog: may every Dog that dies
Lie in security – as this Dog lies.

EPITAPH ON THE POLITICIAN HIMSELF

Here richly, with ridiculous display,
The Politician's corpse was laid away.
While all of his acquaintance sneered and slanged
I wept: for I had longed to see him hanged.

ANOTHER ON THE SAME

This, the last ornament among the peers,
Bribed, bullied, swindled and blackmailed for years:
But Death's what even Politicians fail
To bribe or swindle, bully or blackmail.

ON MUNDANE ACQUAINTANCES

Good morning, Algernon: Good morning, Percy.
Good morning, Mrs Roebeck. Christ have mercy!

ON A ROSE FOR HER BOSOM

Go, lovely rose, and tell the lovelier fair
That he which loved her most was never there.

ON THE LITTLE GOD

Of all the gods that gave me all their glories
To-day there deigns to walk with me but one.
I lead him by the hand and tell him stories.
It is the Queen of Cyprus' little son.

ON A PROPHET

Of old 'twas Samuel sought the Lord: to-day
The Lord runs after Samuel – so they say.

ON A DEAD HOSTESS

Of this bad world the loveliest and the best
Has smiled and said 'Good Night,' and gone to rest.

ON A GENERAL ELECTION

The accursèd power which stands on Privilege
(And goes with Women, and Champagne and Bridge)
Broke – and Democracy resumed her reign:
(Which goes with Bridge, and Women and Champagne).

ON A MISTAKEN MARINER

He whistled thrice to pass the Morning Star,
Thinking that near which was so very far.
So I, whenas I meet my Dearest Dear,
Still think that far which is so very near.

ON A SLEEPING FRIEND

Lady, when your lovely head
Droops to sink among the Dead,
And the quiet places keep
You that so divinely sleep;
Then the dead shall blessèd be
With a new solemnity,
For such Beauty, so descending,
Pledges them that Death is ending.
Sleep your fill – but when you wake
Dawn shall over Lethe break.

FATIGUE

I'm tired of Love: I'm still more tired of Rhyme.
But Money gives me pleasure all the time.

[115]

PARTLY FROM THE GREEK
She would be as the stars in your sight
That turn in the endless hollow;
That tremble, and always follow
The quiet wheels of the Night.

FROM THE SAME
Love's self is sad. Love's lack is sadder still.
But Love unloved, O, that's the greatest ill!

PARTLY FROM THE LATIN
Suns may set and suns may rise,
   Our poor eyes
When their little light is past
   Droop and go to sleep at last.

HER FINAL ROLE
This man's desire; that other's hopeless end;
A third's capricious tyrant: and my friend.

ON EYES
Dark eyes adventure bring; the blue serene
Do promise Paradise: and yours are green.

ON A HAND
Her hand which touched my hand she moved away.
But there it lies, for ever and a day.

OBEAM LIBENS
Insult, despise me; what you can't prevent
Is that my verse shall be your monument.
But, Oh my torment, if you treat me true
I'll cancel every line, for love of you.

[116]

ON THE LADIES OF PIXTON

Three Graces; and the mother were a Grace,
But for profounder meaning in her face.

THE DIAMOND

This diamond, Juliet, will adorn
Ephemeral beauties yet unborn.
While my strong verse, for ever new,
Shall still adorn immortal you.

THE FRAGMENT

Towards the evening of her splendid day
Those who are little children now shall say
(Finding this verse), 'Who wrote it, Juliet?'
And Juliet answer gently, 'I forget.'

ON VITAL STATISTICS

Ill fares the land to hast'ning *ills* a prey[1]
Where wealth accumulates and men decay.'
But how much more unfortunate are those
Where wealth declines and population grows!

CRITERION

When you are mixed with many I descry
A single light, and judge the rest thereby.
But when you are alone with me, why then,
I quite forget all women and all men.

THE FACE

A face Sir Joshua might have painted! Yea:
Sir Joshua painted anything for pay . . .
And after all you're painted every day.

[1] This line is execrable; and I note it.
I quote it as the faulty poet wrote it.

ON A GREAT HOUSE

These are the lawns where Cœlia lived and moved;
Was loved, and lovely was: but never loved.

ON TWO MINISTERS OF STATE

Lump says that Caliban's of gutter breed,
And Caliban says Lump's a fool indeed,
And Caliban and Lump and I are all agreed.

ON CHELSEA

I am assured by Dauber's wife
That Dauber's always true to life.
I think his wife would far prefer
That Dauber should be true to her.

THE PACIFIST

Pale Ebenezer thought it wrong to fight,
But Roaring Bill (who killed him) thought it right.

ON ANOTHER POLITICIAN

The Politician, dead and turned to clay,
Will make a clout to keep the wind away.
I am not fond of draughts, and yet I doubt
If I could get myself to touch that clout.

ON YET ANOTHER

Fame to her darling Shifter glory gives;
And Shifter is immortal, while he lives.

ON A PURITAN

He served his God so faithfully and well
That now he sees him face to face, in hell.

[118]

ON THE LITTLE GOD
The love of God which leads to realms above
Is contre-carréd by the God of Love.

ON A SUNDIAL
In soft deluding lies let fools delight.
A Shadow marks our days; which end in Night.

ON ANOTHER
How slow the Shadow creeps: but when 'tis past
How fast the Shadows fall. How fast! How fast!

ON ANOTHER
Loss and Possession, Death and Life are one.
There falls no shadow where there shines no sun.

ON ANOTHER
Stealthy the silent hours advance, and still;
And each may wound you, and the last shall kill.

ON ANOTHER
Here in a lonely glade, forgotten, I
Mark the tremendous process of the sky.
So does your inmost soul, forgotten, mark
The Dawn, the Noon, the coming of the Dark.

ON ANOTHER
I that still point to one enduring star
Abandoned am, as all the Constant are.

ON ANOTHER
Save on the rare occasions when the Sun
Is shining, I am only here for fun.

ON ANOTHER
I am a sundial, and I make a botch
Of what is done far better by a watch.

ON ANOTHER
I am a sundial, turned the wrong way round.
I cost my foolish mistress fifty pound.

ON A GREAT NAME
I heard to-day Godolphin say
He never gave himself away.
Come, come, Godolphin, scion of kings,
Be generous in little things.

★

Is there any reward?
  I'm beginning to doubt it.
I am broken and bored,
  Is there any reward?
Reassure me, Good Lord,
  And inform me about it.
Is there any reward?
  I'm beginning to doubt it.

HABITATIONS
Kings live in Palaces, and Pigs in sties,
And youth in Expectation. Youth is wise.

ON A HUGE DRINKING VESSEL
King Alfred was in Wantage born;
He drank out of a ram's horn.
Here is a better man than he,
Who drinks deeper, as you see.

*

If all the harm that women do
    Were put into a barrel
And taken out and drowned in Looe
    Why, men would never quarrel!

KINSHIP

Blood is thicker than water –
And so it oughter.

AN UNFORTUNATE LANDFALL

I made my passage through St Alban's Race
And came to anchor in this bloody place.

TALKING OF BAD VERSE

William, you vary greatly in your verse;
Some's none too good, but all the rest is worse.

AN EXAMPLE OF THE SAME

Wine exercises a peculiar charm;
But, taken in excess, does grievous harm.

EPITAPH UPON HIMSELF

Lauda tu Ilarion audacem et splendidum,
Who was always beginning things and never ended 'em.

TIME CURES ALL

It was my shame, and now it is my boast,
That I have loved you rather more than most.

KING'S LAND

Stand thou forever among human Houses,
House of the Resurrection, House of Birth;
House of the rooted hearts and long carouses,
Stand, and be famous over all the Earth.

A MODEST POLITICIAN
Godolphin says he does not wish to swell
The Roll of Fame; and it is just as well.

EPITAPH ON A POLITICIAN
Here William lies, in truth; before he died
For forty mortal years in truth he lied!

★

[. . . 'Hence the motto which a poet engraved upon the inside
of his expensive watch and then transferred to a sundial:']

Ephemeral mortal, mark my emblem well:
I tell the Time, and Time in time will tell.

★

His prose and his verse, and a touch of a curse
Will accompany Hilary up to his Hearse.

ON A SUNDIAL
Creep, shadow, creep: my ageing hours tell.
I cannot stop you, so you may as well.

ON ANOTHER
I am a Sundial. Ordinary words
Cannot express my thoughts on Birds.

BALLADES

Gigantic daughter of the West
   (The phrase is Tennysonian), who
From this unconquerable breast
   The vigorous milk of Freedom drew
– We gave it freely – shall the crest
   Of Empire in your keeping true,
Shall England – I forget the rest,
   But Consols are at 82.

Now why should anyone invest,
   As even City people do
(His Lordship did among the rest),
   When stocks – but what is that to you?
And then, who ever could have guessed
   About the guns – and horses too! –
Besides, they knew their business best,
   And Consols are at 82.

It serves no purpose to protest,
   It isn't manners to halloo
About the way the thing was messed –
   Or vaguely call a man a Jew.
A gentleman who cannot jest
   Remarked that we should muddle through
(The continent was much impressed),
   And Consols are at 82.

Envoi

Prince, Botha lay at Pilgrim's Rest
   And Myberg in the Great Karoo
(A desert to the south and west),
   And Consols are at 82.

[125]

Postscript

Permit me – if you do not mind –
   To add it would be screaming fun
If, after printing this, I find
   Them after all at 81.

Or 70 or 63,
   Or 55 or 44,
Or 39 and going free,
   Or 28 – or even more.

Further Envoi[1]

No matter – take no more advice
   From doubtful and intriguing men.
Refuse the stuff at any price,
   And slowly watch them fall to 10.

Meanwhile I feel a certain zest
   In writing once again the new
Refrain that all is for the best,
   And Consols are at 82.

Last Envoi

Prince, you and I were barely thirty-three,
   And now I muse and wonder if it's true,
That you were you and I myself was me,
   And 3 per cents were really 82!

[1] [The sub-title 'Further Envoi' and the whole of the Last Envoi were added in the 1938 edition.]

What dwelling hath Sir Harland Pott
  That died of drinking in Bungay?
Nathaniel Goacher who was shot
  Towards the end of Malplaquet?
The only thing that we can say
  (The only thing that has been said)
About these gentlemen is 'Nay!'
  But where are the unanswering dead?

Lord Bumplepuppy, too, that got
  The knock from Messrs Dawkins' dray?
And Jonas, whom the Cachalot
  Begulphed in Esdraelon Bay?
The Calvinistic John McKay,
  Who argued till his nostrils bled,
And dropped in apoplexy? Nay!
  But where are the unanswering dead?

And Heliodorus too, that hot
  Defender of the Roman sway;
And He, the author of the 'Tot
  Mercedes dant Victoriæ,'
And all the armoured squadrons gay
  That ever glory nourishèd
In all the world's high charges? Nay!
  But where are the unanswering dead?

Envoi
Prince, have you ever learnt to pray
  Upon you knees beside your bed?
You miserable waxwork? Nay!
  But where are the unanswering dead?

Lady and Queen and Mystery manifold
  And very Regent of the untroubled sky,
Whom in a dream St Hilda did behold
  And heard a woodland music passing by:
  You shall receive me when the clouds are high
With evening and the sheep attain the fold.
This is the faith that I have held and hold,
  And this is that in which I mean to die.

Steep are the seas and savaging and cold
  In broken waters terrible to try;
And vast against the winter night the wold,
  And harbourless for any sail to lie.
  But you shall lead me to the lights, and I
Shall hymn you in a harbour story told.
This is the faith that I have held and hold,
  And this is that in which I mean to die.

Help of the half-defeated, House of Gold,
  Shrine of the Sword, and Tower of Ivory;
Splendour apart, supreme and aureoled,
  The Battler's vision and the World's reply.
  You shall restore me, O my last Ally,
To vengeance and the glories of the bold.
This is the faith that I have held and hold,
  And this is that in which I mean to die.

Envoi

Prince of the degradations, bought and sold,
  These verses, written in your crumbling sty,
Proclaim the faith that I have held and hold
  And publish that in which I mean to die.

I'm going out to dine at Gray's
   With Bertie Morden, Charles and Kit,
And Manderly who never pays,
   And Jane who wins in spite of it,
   And Algernon who won't admit
The truth about his curious hair
   And teeth that very nearly fit: –
And Mrs Roebeck will be there.

And then to-morrow someone says
   That someone else has made a hit
In one of Mister Twister's plays,
   And off we go to yawn at it;
   And when it's petered out we quit
For number 20, Taunton Square,
   And smoke, and drink, and dance a bit: –
And Mrs Roebeck will be there.

And so through each declining phase
   Of emptied effort, jaded wit,
And day by day of London days
   Obscurely, more obscurely, lit;
   Until the uncertain shadows flit
Announcing to the shuddering air
   A Darkening, and the end of it: –
And Mrs Roebeck will be there.

Envoi
Prince, on their iron thrones they sit,
   Impassable to our despair,
The dreadful Guardians of the Pit: –
   And Mrs Roebeck will be there.

The cause of all the poor in '93:
  The cause of all the world at Waterloo:
The shouts of what was terrible and free
  Behind the guns of *Vengeance* and her crew:
The Maid that rode so straightly and so true
  And broke the line to pieces in her pride –
They had to chuck it up; it wouldn't do;
  The Devil didn't like them, and they died.

Cæsar and Alexander shall agree
  That right athwart the world their bugles blew:
And all the lads that marched in Lombardy
  Behind the young Napoleon charging through:
All that were easy swordsmen, all that slew
  The Monsters, and that served our God and tried
The temper of this world – they lost the clue.
  The Devil didn't like them, and they died.

You, the strong sons of anger and the sea,
  What darkness on the wings of battle flew?
Then the great dead made answer: 'Also we
  With Nelson found oblivion: Nelson, who
When cheering out of port in spirit grew
  To make one purpose with the wind and tide –
Our nameless hulks are sunk and rotted through:
  The Devil didn't like us and we died.'

Envoi

Prince, may I venture (since it's only you)
  To speak discreetly of The Crucified?
He was extremely unsuccessful too:
  The Devil didn't like Him, and He died.

[130]

John Calvin whose peculiar fad
  It was to call God murderous,
Which further led that feverish cad
  To burn alive the Servetus.
The horrible Bohemian Huss,
  The tedious Wycliffe, where are they?
But where is old Nestorius?
  The wind has blown them all away.

The Kohen out of Novdograd
  Who argued from the Roman Jus
'Privata fasta nihil ad
  Rem nisi sint de sacribus.'
And Hume, who made a dreadful fuss
  About the Resurrection Day
And said it was ridiculous –
  The wind has blown them all away.

Of Smith the gallant Mormon lad
  That took of wives an over-plus:
Johanna Southcott who was mad
  And nasty Nietzsche, who was worse.
Of Tolstoy, the Eccentric Russ,
  Our strong Posterity shall say:
'Lord Jesus! What are these to us?
  The wind has blown them all away!'

Envoi

Prince, should you meet upon a bus
  A man who makes a great display
Of Dr Haeckel, argue thus: –
  The wind has blown them all away.

The other day the £ fell out of bed
With consequences that are far from clear;
For instance, Eldorado Deeps, instead
Of jumping up, incline to lurch and veer;
And while Commander Turtle thinks it queer
Professor Guff is willing to explain;
But anyhow, the quiet profiteer
Will miss the Riviera and Champagne.

The out o'work will miss his loaf of bread,
The half-at-work will miss his glass of beer,
The City clerk – who might as well be dead –
Will miss the slight advance in his career,
And very many of my friends, I fear,
(Like Algernon, who hasn't got a brain)
A-pacing hollow-eyed on Brighton Pier,
Will miss the Riviera and Champagne.

Ladies and Lords who once on glory fed,
Renaldo, Pharamond and Guinevere,
And Francis, that in glittering armour led
The long defile of Lance and Halberdier;
High Captains of an elder world, give ear –
Cæsar and Bonaparte and Charlemagne –
The nobler masters of our modern sphere
Will miss the Riviera and Champagne.

Envoi
Prince, Oh my Prince, 'Tis heavenly to hear!
Stroke the piano; croon it once again . . .
'The Rich, the Very Rich, this very year,
Will miss the Riviera and Champagne.'

BALLADE OF ILLEGAL ORNAMENTS

'. . . the controversy was ended by His Lordship, who wrote to
the Incumbent ordering him to remove from the Church all Illegal
Ornaments at once, and especially a Female Figure with a Child.'

When that the Eternal deigned to look
    On us poor folk to make us free,
He chose a Maiden, whom He took
    From Nazareth in Galilee;
    Since when the Islands of the Sea,
The Field, the City, and the Wild
    Proclaim aloud triumphantly
A Female Figure with a Child.

These Mysteries profoundly shook
    The Reverend Doctor Leigh, D.D.,
Who therefore stuck into a Nook
    (or Niche) of his Incumbency
    An Image filled with majesty
To represent the Undefiled,
    The Universal Mother – She –
A Female Figure with a Child.

His Bishop, having read a book
    Which proved as plain as plain could be
That all the Mutts had been mistook
    Who talked about a Trinity,
    Wrote off at once to Doctor Leigh
In manner very far from mild,
    And said: 'Remove them instantly!
A Female Figure with a Child!'

Envoi

Prince Jesus, in mine Agony,
    Permit me, broken and defiled,
Through blurred and glazing eyes to see
    A Female Figure with a Child.

[133]

An expert in tobacco – to be terse
A traveller for Mr William Wrenn –
Assured me (as I fiddled with my purse,
To pay for drinks which he had ordered when
I met him years ago in Tenterden)
That if you have a lot of smokes to sell
The outer leaf is everything, and then
It is the covers of cigars that tell.

It is indeed! Oh Dark Primordial Curse!
(I cannot think of any rhyme but 'hen',
Nor after that of anything but 'hearse',
Nor after that of anything but 'fen',
Nor – now I have it! –) Louder than Big Ben
I hear the challenge of unconquered Hell
Call from the limits of our human ken:
'It is the covers of cigars that tell.'

Readers, oh readers, readers of my verse,
I wish I hadn't taken up my pen.
The stuff to come will probably be worse
Than – readers, oh my readers (once again!) . . .
My brain is empty. It is half-past ten,
And somebody is ringing at the bell: –
But here's a message to my fellow men:
It is the covers of cigars that tell.

Envoi

Prince, certain not exactly gentlemen
Have boasted your acquaintance. Very well:
So be it: There's an end of it: Amen.
It is the covers of cigars that tell.

My reading is extremely deep and wide;
And as our modern education goes –
Unique I think, and skilfully applied
To Art and Industry and *Autres Choses*
Through many years of scholarly repose.
But there is one thing where I disappoint
My numerous admirers (and my foes).
Painting on Vellum is my weakest point.

I ride superbly. When I say I 'ride'
The word's too feeble. I am one of those
That dominate a horse. It is my pride
To tame the fiercest with tremendous blows
Of heel and knee. The while my handling shows
Such lightness as a lady's. But Aroint
Thee! Human frailty with thy secret woes!
Painting on Vellum is my weakest point.

Painting on Vellum: not on silk or hide
Or ordinary Canvas: I suppose
No painter of the present day has tried
So many mediums with success, or knows
As well as I do how the subject grows
Beneath the hands of genius, that anoint
With balm. But I have something to disclose –
Painting on Vellum is my weakest point.

Envoi

Prince! do not let your Nose, your royal Nose,
Your large imperial Nose get out of Joint.
For though you cannot touch my golden Prose,
Painting on Vellum is my weakest point.

Shooting one day with other people in
A wood called Archers on the Upper Clyde,
I caught a certain Scotchman on the shin
From aiming rather blindly down the ride.
It wounded him – not only in his pride –
And ever since he goes a trifle lame:
And when I meet him now I run and hide.
I fear that I was more or less to blame.

In Norfolk, in the ancient town of Lynn,
I brought up sharply, on a racing tide,
A lovely little yawl, which to begin
With wasn't mine: that cannot be denied.
A man had lent it me. And, as I tried
To pick up moorings and make fast the same,
I caught a post which smashed her starboard side.
I fear that I was more or less to blame.

Another time, when I was keen to win
A friend a by-election, I applied
To both the Central Offices for tin,
And by judicious hints of trouble guyed
Them *both* into disbursing loose and wide.
Well. Politics is a disgusting game,
But still – how monumentally I lied!
I fear that I was more or less to blame.

Envoi
Prince, when you caught that little butter-slide
Against the Palace, *what* a smack you came!
Laugh? Bless your soul! I thought I should have *died*
. . . I fear that I was more or less to blame.

[136]

Some time ago a tall Romantic Pole
Called Mr Montagueski (whom I met
By accident when taking of a stroll
At Lord's where he was bowling in a net),
Informed me unexpectedly his pet
Reminder was, and had been many a day:
A Royalty is something which you get
For which another Person has to pay.

Thereat I told him that a heavy toll
Is levied by the Haughty Blokes in Brett
And Burke and other people on the roll
Of Parliament and all that sort of set
Upon the common Tonnage, tare and tret,
Of Coal, Chalk, Bread, Air, Water, Beer, and Clay –
A Royalty is something which you get
For which another Person has to pay.

Books have their Royalties as well as Coal
(And precious measly little things, you bet!).
Successful authors find upon the whole
That getting very deeply into debt
Is less expensive than the dreadful fret
Of waiting, waiting, waiting for the day –
A Royalty is something that you get
For which another Person has to pay.

Envoi
Prince, when you went and stopped in Somerset,
At Algernon's, I heard his sister say,
'A Royalty is something that you get
For which another person has to pay.'

[137]

We might have heard great Homer in a hall,
  Some three and thirty centuries ago,
Tune carefully at first and then recall
    Upon his harp what now the nations know
    To their enlargement; and with cheeks aglow
We might have left this presence, Helené,
  And Paris would have been my name – but No,
Fate wished it otherwise with you and me.

We might have kept a dirty little stall
  Of whelks and periwinkles in Soho,
And made a doubtful living there withal,
    But made a living anyhow – and Oh!
    Not ever suffered from that to and fro,
Which very nearly wrecked our jollity.
  We might have really worked and loved – but No!
Fate wished it otherwise with you and me.

We might have followed that remembered wall,
  Which dips into the river by Lerraulx,
Rich with large blooms and silence magical
    And deep as youth, and as youth's season slow,
    And budding gardens where today there glow
Those fruits we lost on the forbidden tree.
  Great God! The thirst for timeless joys! But No,
Fate wished it otherwise with you and me.

Envoi

Prince, it would hugely gratify my toe
To kick you all the way to Bermondsey,
  Did cogent public powers allow – but No!
Fate wished it otherwise with you and me.

[138]

The greater part of all the food you eat
  Is chemically poisoned! That is so.
You sicken upon very doubtful meat;
    Your beer is made, I am prepared to show,
    Of SO$_3$, with too much H$_2$O,
And that's the reason you have stomach-cold.
    But these are things that people do not know;
They do not know because they are not told.

There is Proclynasis as well as wheat
    And harmless Alum in the baker's dough;
Your salt is made from sweepings of the street
    The while the peer who sells it you (what ho!)
    Presides by statute over that Bureau
Which legally allows it to be sold:
    But these are things that people do not know;
They do not know because they are not told.

So grin and bear it, Stupid, do not bleat;
    You hungered after progress years ago;
You wanted science and you've got it – neat;
    You certainly desired 'Hygiene' and lo!
    You have it now – and mutter in your woe
Of bitter knowledge dearer bought than gold.
    'These are the things that people do not know;
They do not know because they are not told.'

Envoi
    Prince, have you seen the funny things they grow,
To make Your Majesty's Champagne – but hold!
    These are the things that people do not know;
They do not know because they are not told.

A child at Brighton has been left to drown:
   A railway train has jumped the line at Crewe:
I haven't got the change for half a crown:
   I can't imagine what on earth to do . . .
   Three bisons have stampeded from the Zoo.
A German fleet has anchored in the Clyde.
   By God the wretched country's up the flue!
– The ice is breaking up on every side.

What! Further news? Rhodesian stocks are down?
   England, my England, can the news be true!
Cannot the Duke be got to come to town?
   Or will not Mr Hooper pull us through?
   And now the Bank is stopping payment too,
The chief cashier has cut his throat and died,
   And Scotland Yard has failed to find a clue:
– The ice is breaking up on every side.

A raging mob inflamed by Charley Brown
   Is tearing up the rails of Waterloo;
They've hanged the Chancellor in wig and gown,
   The Speaker, and the Chief Inspector too!
   Police! Police! Is this the road to Kew?
I can't keep up: my garter's come untied:
   I shall be murdered by the savage crew.
– The ice is breaking up on every side.

Envoi

Prince of the Empire, Prince of Timbuctoo,
Prince eight feet round and nearly four feet wide,
   Do try to run a little faster, do.
– The ice is breaking up on every side.

Companions of the darkness, all you planned
  Has whispered into nothingness and fled
To mix with empty night. The groping hand
  Has caught no holding, nor the eye no shred
  Of lifting dawn at last; but in its stead
The viewless Power is on us: and it fills
  The stark inane with fixity and dread .
– I wish to God that I could pay my bills.

All the new Angers in the swelling band
  Of men grown desperate – like poor old Fred
Who hanged himself at home, I understand,
  To save a scandal – in the motor shed.
  As I was saying, all must turn and tread
Whatever Pathway the one Purpose wills,
  Which hath the Heavens in Iron Order spread
– I wish to God that I could pay my bills!

Yet, Freedom, in the mountains where you stand
  Triumphant with that wind about your head
Of the High Places and inviolate land –
  There have I mingled with you, nourishéd
  Upon your substance as upon a bread
Of tireless hope, and drunken of the rills
  From barren but unconquered moorlands fed!
– I wish to God that I could pay my bills.

Envoi
  Prince, you have heard about the Child who said
'My name is Norval! On the Grampian Hills
  My Father kept his flocks'? That Child is dead.
– I wish to God that I could pay my bills.

[141]

BALLADE OF GENTLEMANLY FEELING
AND RAILWAY STRIKES

Nothing is more ungentlemanly than
   Exaggeration, causing needless pain:
It's worse than spitting, and it stamps a man
   Deservedly with other men's disdain.
   Weigh human actions carefully. Explain
The worst of them with charity. Mayhap
   There were two sides to that affair of Cain –
And Judas was a tolerable chap!

This sort of recklessness has laid a ban
   (Most properly!) upon the works of Paine;
And should in decency condemn the clan
   Of mean detractors, like the half-insane
   And filthy Swift, Elijah, and again
The hare-brained Dante, with his snarl and yap –
   No life, however warped, was lived in vain.
And Judas was a tolerable chap.

Benedict Arnold doubtless had a plan
   For profiting his country: it is plain
That nothing but the voice of slander can
   Have poisoned such a man as Charlemagne
   Against the martyred Ganelon in Spain.
We know that Dreyfus fell into a trap –
   Which also may be true of poor Bazaine –
And Judas was a tolerable chap.

Envoi
Prince, even you are hardly so inane
As not to understand the sad mishap
   Befallen those who run the railway-train –
And Judas was a tolerable chap.

Having to write a Ballade I commence –
 Or, as the English of it does – begin
Urbanely: London, an inane immense
 Of poverty anarchic, dull with gin,
 Fallen too far for hope or discipline,
Sprawling a waste of dirty lanes and quays,
 And dust and most intolerable din: –
– But what have I to do with all of these?

The suburbs as a whole, and their intense
 And aching void of End and Origin:
The wicked little strips of lattice fence:
 The starved religion, formal, lean and thin.
 The miserable sheds of painted tin:
Gaunt Villas, planted round with stunted trees
 And, God! the dreadful things that dwell therein!
– But what have I to do with all of these?

The Provinces: the way they judge in pence
 And pounds and shillings, and the way they pin
Their souls to title: solid insolence;
 Self-satisfaction with its odious grin:
 Walled ignorance contented, and again,
Elderly women full of Mignardises –
 The latest fruit of Adam's ancient sin –
But what have I to do with all of these?

Envoi
 Prince, Orders might as well be made of tin
Yet will the Bosses waddle on their knees,
 Fat rogues and old, such ornaments to win;
But what have I to do with all of these?

[143]

SATIRES IMITATIONS & GROTESQUES

THE JUSTICE OF THE PEACE

Distinguish carefully between these two,
  This thing is yours, that other thing is mine.
You have a shirt, a brimless hat, a shoe
  And half a coat. I am the Lord benign
Of fifty hundred acres of fat land
To which I have a right. You understand?

I have a right because I have, because,
  Because I have – because I have a right.
Now be quite calm and good, obey the laws,
  Remember your low station, do not fight
Against the goad, because, you know, it pricks
Whenever the uncleanly demos kicks.

I do not envy you your hat, your shoe.
  Why should you envy me my small estate?
It's fearfully illogical in you
  To fight with economic force and fate.
Moreover, I have got the upper hand,
And mean to keep it. Do you understand?

TO DIVES

Dives, when you and I go down to Hell,
Where scribblers end and millionaires as well,
We shall be carrying on our separate backs
Two very large but very different packs;
And as you stagger under yours, my friend,
Down the dull shore where all our journeys end,
And go before me (as your rank demands)
Towards the infinite flat underlands,
And that dear river of forgetfulness –

Charon, a man of exquisite address
(For, as your wife's progenitors could tell,
They're very strict on etiquette in Hell).
Will, since you are a lord, observe, 'My lord,
We cannot take these weighty things aboard!'
Then down they go, my wretched Dives, down –
The fifteen sorts of boots you kept for town;
The hat to meet the Devil in; the plain
But costly ties; the cases of champagne;
The solid watch, and seal, and chain, and charm;
The working model of a Burning Farm
(To give the little Belials); all the three
Biscuits for Cerberus; the guarantee
From Lambeth that the Rich can never burn,
And even promising a safe return;
The admirable overcoat, designed
To cross Cocytus – very warmly lined:
Sweet Dives, you will leave them all behind
And enter Hell as tattered and as bare
As was your father when he took the air
Behind a barrow-load in Leicester Square.
Then turned to me, and noting one that brings
With careless step a mist of shadowy things:
Laughter and memories, and a few regrets,
Some honour, and a quantity of debts,
A doubt or two of sorts, a trust in God,
And (what will seem to you extremely odd)
His father's granfer's father's father's name,
Unspoilt, untitled, even spelt the same;
Charon, who twenty thousand times before
Has ferried Poets to the ulterior shore,
Will estimate the weight I bear, and cry –
'Comrade!' (He has himself been known to try
His hand at Latin and Italian verse,
Much in the style of Virgil – only worse)

[148]

'We let such vain imaginaries pass!'
Then tell me, Dives, which will look the ass –
You, or myself? Or Charon? Who can tell?
They order things so damnably in Hell.

THE FANATIC

Last night in Compton Street, Soho,
A man whom many of you know
Gave up the ghost at half past nine.
That evening he had been to dine
At Gressington's – an act unwise,
But not the cause of his demise.
The doctors all agree that he
Was touched with cardiac atrophy
Accelerated (more or less)
By lack of proper food, distress,
Uncleanliness, and loss of sleep.
    He was a man that could not keep
His money (when he had the same)
Because of creditors who came
And took it from him; and he gave
So freely that he could not save.
    But all the while a sort of whim
Persistently remained with him,
Half admirable, half absurd:
To keep his word, to keep his word . . .
By which he did not mean what you
And I would mean (of payments due
Or punctual rental of the Flat –
He was a deal too mad for that)
But – as he put it with a fine
Abandon, foolish or divine –
But 'That great word which every man

Gave God before his life began.'
It was a sacred word, he said,
Which comforted the pathless dead
And made God smile when it was shown
Unforfeited, before the Throne.
And this (he said) he meant to hold
In spite of debt, and hate, and cold;
And this (he said) he meant to show
As passport to the Wards below.
He boasted of it and gave praise
To his own self through all his days.

He wrote a record to preserve
How steadfastly he did not swerve
From keeping it; how stiff he stood
Its guardian, and maintained it good.
He had two witnesses to swear
He kept it once in Berkeley Square
(Where hardly anything survives),
And, through the loneliest of lives
He kept it clean, he kept it still,
Down to the last extremes of ill.

So when he died, of many friends
Who came in crowds from all the ends
Of London, that it might be known
They knew the man who died alone,
Some, who had thought his mood sublime
And sent him soup from time to time,
Said, 'Well, you cannot make them fit
The world, and there's an end of it!'
But others, wondering at him, said:
The man that kept his word is dead!'

Then angrily, a certain third
Cried, 'Gentlemen, he kept his word.
And as a man whom beasts surround
Tumultuous, on a little mound

Stands Archer, for one dreadful hour,
Because a Man is born to Power –
And still, to daunt the pack below,
Twangs the clear purpose of his bow,
Till overwhelmed he dares to fall:
So stood this bulwark of us all.
He kept his word as none but he
Could keep it, and as did not we.
And round him as he kept his word
Today's diseased and faithless herd,
A moment loud, a moment strong,
But foul forever, rolled along.'

You thought because we held, my lord,
    An ancient cause and strong,
That therefore we maligned the sword:
    My lord, you did us wrong.

We also know the sacred height
    Up on Tugela side,
Where those three hundred fought with Beit
    And fair young Wernher died.

The daybreak on the failing force,
    The final sabres drawn:
Tall Goltman, silent on his horse,
    Superb against the dawn.

[151]

The little mound where Eckstein stood
  And gallant Albu fell,
And Oppenheim, half blind with blood,
Went fording through the rising flood –
  My Lord, we know them well.

The little empty homes forlorn,
The ruined synagogues that mourn,
  In Frankfort and Berlin;
We knew them when the peace was torn –
We of a nobler lineage born –
And now by all the gods of scorn
  We mean to rub them in.

THE HAPPY JOURNALIST

I love to walk about at night
  By nasty lanes and corners foul,
All shielded from the unfriendly light
  And independent as the owl.

By dirty grates I love to lurk;
  I often stoop to take a squint
At printers working at their work.
  I muse upon the rot they print.

The beggars please me, and the mud:
  The editors beneath their lamps
As – Mr Howl demanding blood,
  And Lord Retender stealing stamps,

And Mr Bing instructing liars,
  His elder son composing trash;
Beaufort (whose real name is Meyers)
  Refusing anything but cash.

I like to think of Mr Meyers,
  I like to think of Mr Bing.
I like to think about the liars:
  It pleases me, that sort of thing.

Policemen speak to me, but I,
  Remembering my civic rights,
Neglect them and do not reply.
  I love to walk about at nights!

At twenty-five to four I bunch
  Across a cab I can't afford.
I ring for breakfast after lunch.
  I am as happy as a lord!

LINES TO A DON

Remote and ineffectual Don
That dared attack my Chesterton,
With that poor weapon, half-impelled,
Unlearnt, unsteady, hardly held,
Unworthy for a tilt with men –
Your quavering and corroded pen;
Don poor at Bed and worse at Table,
Don pinched, Don starved, Don miserable;
Don stuttering, Don with roving eyes,
Don nervous, Don of crudities;
Don clerical, Don ordinary,
Don self-absorbed and solitary;
Don here-and-there, Don epileptic;
Don puffed and empty, Don dyspeptic;
Don middle-class, Don sycophantic,
Don dull, Don brutish, Don pedantic;

[153]

Don hypocritical, Don bad,
Don furtive, Don three-quarters mad;
Don (since a man must make an end),
Don that shall never be my friend.

.   .   .

Don different from those regal Dons!
With hearts of gold and lungs of bronze,
Who shout and bang and roar and bawl
The Absolute across the hall,
Or sail in amply billowing gown
Enormous through the Sacred Town,
Bearing from College to their homes
Deep cargoes of gigantic tomes;
Dons admirable! Dons of Might!
Uprising on my inward sight
Compact of ancient tales, and port
And sleep – and learning of a sort.
Dons English, worthy of the land;
Dons rooted; Dons that understand.
Good Dons perpetual that remain
A landmark, walling in the plain –
The horizon of my memories –
Like large and comfortable trees.

.   .   .

Don very much apart from these,
Thou scapegoat Don, thou Don devoted,
Don to thine own damnation quoted,
Perplexed to find thy trivial name
Reared in my verse to lasting shame.
Don dreadful, rasping Don and wearing,
Repulsive Don – Don past all bearing.

Don of the cold and doubtful breath,
Don despicable, Don of death;
Don nasty, skimpy, silent, level;
Don evil; Don that serves the devil.
Don ugly – that makes fifty lines.
There is a Canon which confines
A Rhymed Octosyllabic Curse
If written in Iambic Verse
To fifty lines. I never cut;
I far prefer to end it – but
Believe me I shall soon return.
My fires are banked, but still they burn
To write some more about the Don
That dared attack my Chesterton.

NEWDIGATE POEM

A PRIZE POEM SUBMITTED BY MR LAMBKIN,
THEN SCHOLAR AND LATER FELLOW OF BURFORD COLLEGE,
TO THE EXAMINERS OF THE UNIVERSITY OF OXFORD
ON THE PRESCRIBED POETIC THEME SET BY THEM IN 1893.
'THE BENEFITS OF THE ELECTRIC LIGHT'

Hail, Happy Muse, and touch the tuneful string!
The benefits conferred by Science[1] I sing.
    Under the kind Examiners' direction[2]
I only write about them in connection
With benefits which the Electric Light
Confers on us; especially at night.
These are my theme, of these my song shall rise.

[1] To be pronounced as a monosyllable in the Imperial fashion.
[2] Mr Punt, Mr Howl, and Mr Grewcock (now, alas, deceased).

My lofty head shall swell to strike the skies.[1]
And tears of hopeless love bedew the maiden's eyes.
    Descend, O Muse, from thy divine abode,
    To Osney, on the Seven Bridges Road;
For under Osney's solitary shade
The bulk of the Electric Light is made.
Here are the works; – from hence the current flows
Which (so the Company's prospectus goes)
    Can furnish to Subscribers hour by hour
No less than sixteen thousand candle power,[2]
All at a thousand volts. (It is essential
To keep the current at this high potential
In spite of the considerable expense.)
    The Energy developed represents,
Expressed in foot-tons, the united forces
Of fifteen elephants and forty horses.
But shall my scientific detail thus
Clip the dear wings of Buoyant Pegasus?
    Shall pure statistics jar upon the ear
That pants for Lyric accents loud and clear?
Shall I describe the complex Dynamo
Or write about its Commutator? No!
    To happier fields I lead my wanton pen,
The proper study of mankind is men.
    Awake, my Muse! Portray the pleasing sight
That meets us where they make Electric Light.
    Behold the Electrician where he stands:
Soot, oil, and verdigris are on his hands;
Large spots of grease defile his dirty clothes,
The while his conversation drips with oaths.
Shall such a being perish in its youth?
Alas! it is indeed the fatal truth.

[1] A neat rendering of 'Sublimi feriam sidera vertice.'
[2] To the Examiners: These facts (of which I guarantee the accuracy) were given me by a Director.

In that dull brain, beneath that hair unkempt,
Familiarity has bred contempt.
We warn him of the gesture all too late:
Oh, Heartless Jove! Oh, Adamantine Fate!

    A random touch – a hand's imprudent slip –
The Terminals – a flash – a sound like 'Zip!'
A smell of burning fills the startled Air –
The Electrician is no longer there!

    But let us turn with true Artistic scorn
From facts funereal and from views forlorn
Of Erebus and blackest midnight born.[1]

    Arouse thee, Muse! and chaunt in accents rich
The interesting processes by which
The Electricity is passed along:
These are my theme: to these I bend my song.

    It runs encased in wood or porous brick
Through copper wires two millimetres thick,
And insulated on their dangerous mission
By indiarubber, silk, or composition.
Here you may put with critical felicity
The following question: 'What is Electricity?'

    'Molecular Activity,' say some,
Others when asked say nothing, and are dumb.
Whatever be its nature, this is clear:
The rapid current checked in its career,
Baulked in its race and halted in its course[2]
Transforms to heat and light its latent force:

    It needs no pedant in the lecturer's chair
To prove that light and heat are present there.
The pear-shaped vacuum globe, I understand,
Is far too hot to fondle with the hand.

[1] A reminiscence of Milton: 'Fas est et ab hoste doceri.'
[2] Lambkin told me he regretted this line, which was for the sake
of Rhyme. He would willingly have replaced it, but to his last
day could construct no substitute.

While, as is patent to the meanest sight,
The carbon filament is very bright.
      As for the lights they hang about the town,
Some praise them highly, others run them down.
This system (technically called the Arc)
Makes some passages too light, others too dark.
      But in the house the soft and constant rays
Have always met with universal praise.
      For instance: if you want to read in bed
No candle burns beside your curtain's head,
For from some distant corner of the room
The incandescent lamp dispels the gloom,
And with the largest print need hardly try
The powers of any young and vigorous eye.
      Aroint thee, Muse! Inspired the poet sings!
I cannot help observing future things!
Life is a vale, its paths are dark and rough
Only because we do not know enough:
When Science has discovered something more
We shall be happier than we were before.
      Hail, Britain, Mistress of the Azure Main,
Ten thousand Fleets sweep over thee in vain!
Hail, Mighty Mother of the Brave and Free,
That beat Napoleon, and gave birth to me!
Thou that canst wrap in thine emblazoned robe
One quarter of the habitable globe.
Thy mountains, wafted by a favouring breeze,
Like mighty rocks withstand the stormy seas.
      Thou art a Christian Commonwealth; and yet
Be thou not all unthankful – nor forget
As thou exultest in Imperial Might
The Benefits of the Electric Light.

THE YELLOW MUSTARD

Oh! ye that prink it to and fro,
In pointed flounce and furbelow,
What have ye known, what can ye know
That have not seen the mustard grow?

The yellow mustard is no less
Than God's good gift to loneliness;
And he was sent in gorgeous press
To jangle keys at my distress.

I heard the throstle call again,
Come thither, Pain! come hither, Pain!
Till all my shameless feet were fain
To wander through the summer rain.

And far apart from human place,
And flaming like a vast disgrace,
There struck me blinding in the face
The livery of the mustard race.

.   .   .

To see the yellow mustard grow
Beyond the town, above, below;
Beyond the purple houses, oh!
To see the yellow mustard grow!

THE POLITICIAN OR THE IRISH EARLDOM

A strong and striking Personality,
    Worth several hundred thousand pounds –
Of strict political Morality –
    Was walking in his park-like Grounds;

[159]

When, just as these began to pall on him
    (I mean the Trees, and Things like that),
A Person who had come to call on him
    Approached him, taking off his Hat.

He said, with singular veracity:
    'I serve our Sea-girt Mother-Land
In no conspicuous capacity.
    I am but an Attorney; and
I do a little elementary
    Negotiation, now and then,
As Agent for a Parliamentary
    Division of the Town of N . . .

'Merely as one of the Electorate –
    A member of the Commonweal –
Before completing my Directorate,
    I want to know the way you feel
On matters more or less debatable;
    As – whether our Imperial Pride
Can treat as taxable or rateable
    The Gardens of . . .' His host replied:

The Ravages of Inebriety
    (Alas! increasing day by day!)
Are undermining all Society.
    I do not hesitate to say
My country squanders her abilities,
    Observe how Montenegro treats
Her Educational Facilities . . .
    . . . As to the African defeats,

'I bitterly deplored their frequency;
    On Canada we are agreed,
The Laws protecting Public Decency
    Are very, very lax indeed!
The Views of most of the Nobility
    Are very much the same as mine,
On Thingumbob's eligibility . . .
    I trust that you remain to dine?'

His Lordship pressed with importunity,
    As rarely he had pressed before.

            .   .   .

    It gave them both an opportunity
    To know each other's value more.

THE LOSER

He lost his money first of all
    – And losing that is half the story –
And later on he tried a fall
    With Fate, in things less transitory.

He lost his heart – and found it dead –
    (His one and only true discovery),
And after that he lost his head,
    And lost his chances of recovery.

He lost his honour bit by bit
    Until the thing was out of question.
He worried so at losing it,
    He lost his sleep and his digestion.

[161]

He lost his temper – and for good –
    The remnants of his reputation,
His taste in wine, his choice of food,
    And then, in rapid culmination,

His certitudes, his sense of truth,
    His memory, his self-control,
The love that graced his early youth,
    And lastly his immortal soul.

STREPHON'S SONG
FROM 'THE CRUEL SHEPHERDESS'

When I was not much older
Than Cupid, but bolder,
I asked of his Mother in passing her bower
What it was in their blindness
Men asked of her kindness
And she said it was nought but a delicate flower:
Such a delicate, delicate, delicate flower!

This morning you kissed me,
By noon you dismissed me
As though such great things were the jest of one hour,
And you left me still wondering
If I were not too blundering
To deal with that delicate, delicate flower:
'Tis such a delicate, delicate, delicate flower!

For if that's the complexion
Of Ladies' affection
I must needs be a fool to remain in their power;

But there's that in me burning
Which brings me returning
To beg for the delicate, delicate flower;
To implore for that delicate, delicate flower!

★

The world's a stage. The light is in one's eyes.
The Auditorium is extremely dark.
The more dishonest get the larger rise;
The more offensive make the greater mark.
The women on it prosper by their shape,
Some few by their vivacity. The men,
By tailoring in breeches and in cape.
The world's a stage – I say it once again.

The scenery is very much the best
Of what the wretched drama has to show,
Also the prompter happens to be dumb,
We drink kehind the scenes and pass a jest
On all our folly; then, before we go
Loud cries for 'Author' . . . but he doesn't come.

★

The world's a stage – and I'm the Super man,
And no one seems responsible for salary.
I roar my part as loudly as I can
And all I mouth I mouth it to the gallery.
I haven't got another rhyme in 'alery';
It would have made a better job, no doubt,
If I had left attempt at Rhyming out,
Like Alfred Tennyson adapting Malory.

[163]

The world's a stage, the company of which
Has very little talent and less reading:
But many a waddling heathen painted bitch
And many a standing cad of gutter breeding.
　　We sweat to learn our book: for all our pains
　　We pass. The Chucker-out alone remains.

　　　　　　　　★

The world's a stage. The trifling entrance fee
Is paid (by proxy) to the registrar.
The Orchestra is very loud and free
But plays no music in particular.
They do not print a programme, that I know.
The cast is large. There isn't any plot.
The acting of the piece is far below
The very worst of modernistic rot.

The only part about it I enjoy
Is what was called in English the Foyay.
There will I stand apart awhile and toy
With thought, and set my cigarette alight;
And then – without returning to the play –
On with my coat and out into the night.

　　　　　　　　★

Would that I had £300,000
　　Invested in some strong security;
A Midland Country House with formal grounds,
　　A Town House, and a House beside the sea,
And one in Spain, and one in Normandy,
　　And Friends innumerable at my call
And youth serene – and underneath it all
　　One steadfast, passionate flame to nurture me.

Then would I chuck for good my stinking trade
  Of writing tosh at 1s. 6d. a quire!
And soar like young Bellerophon arrayed
  High to the filmy Heavens of my desire . . .
    But that's all over. Here's the world again.
    Bring me the Blotter. Fill the fountain-pen.

THE MODERN TRAVELLER

I

The *Daily Menace*, I presume?
Forgive the litter in the room.
I can't explain to you
How out of place a man like me
Would be without the things you see –
The Shields and Assegais and odds
And ends of little savage gods.
Be seated; take a pew.
(Excuse the phrase. I'm rather rough,
And – pardon me! – but have you got
A pencil? I've another here:
The one that you have brought, I fear,
Will not be long enough.)
And so the Public want to hear
About the expedition
From which I recently returned:
Of how the Fetish Tree was burned;
Of how we struggled to the coast,
And lost our ammunition;
How we retreated, side by side;
And how, like Englishmen, we died.

Well, as you know, I hate to boast,
And, what is more, I can't abide
A popular position.
I told the Duke the other day
The way I felt about it.
He answered courteously – 'Oh!'
An Editor (who had an air
Of what the Dutch call *savoir faire*)
Said, 'Mr Rooter, you are right,
And nobody can doubt it.'
The Duchess murmured, 'Very true.'
Her comments may be brief and few,
But very seldom trite.
Still, representing as you do
A public and a point of view,
I'll give you leave to jot
A few remarks – a very few –
But understand that this is not
A formal interview.
And first of all, I will begin
By talking of Commander Sin.

II

Poor Henry Sin from quite a child,
I fear, was always rather wild;
    But all his faults were due
To something free and unrestrained,
That partly pleased and partly pained
    The people whom he knew.
Untaught (for what our times require),
Lazy, and something of a liar,
    He had a foolish way
Of always swearing (more or less);

And, lastly, let us say
A little slovenly in dress,
A trifle prone to drunkenness;
A gambler also to excess,
	And never known to pay.
As for his clubs in London, he
Was pilled at ten, expelled from three.
A man Bohemian as could be –
	But really vicious? Oh, no!
When these are mentioned, all is said.
And then – Commander Sin is dead:
	De Mortuis cui bono?

Of course, the Public know I mean
To publish in the winter.
I mention the intention in
Connection with Commander Sin;
	The book is with the Printer.
And here, among the proofs, I find
The very thing I had in mind –
The portrait upon page thirteen.
Pray pause awhile, and mark
The wiry limbs, the vigorous mien,
The tangled hair and dark;
The glance imperative and hot,
	That takes a world by storm:
All these are in the plate, but what
You chiefly should observe is
The – Did you say his uniform
Betrayed a foreign service?

Of course, it does! He was not born
In little England! No!
Beyond the Cape, beyond the Horn,

Beyond Fernando Po,
In some far Isle he saw the light
That burns the torrid zone,
But where it lay was never quite
Indubitably known.
Himself inclined to Martinique,
His friends to Farralone.
But why of this discussion speak?
The Globe was all his own!
Oh! surely upon such a birth
No petty flag unfurled!
He was a citizen of earth,
A subject of the world!

As for the uniform he bore,
He won it in the recent war
Between Peru and Ecuador,
        And thoroughly he earned it.
Alone of all who at the time
Were serving sentences for crime,
Sin, during his incarceration,
Had studied works on navigation;
And when the people learned it,
They promptly let him out of jail,
But on condition he should sail.

It marked an epoch, and you may
Recall the action in
A place called Quaxipotle bay?
Yes, both the navies ran away;
And yet, if Ecuador can say
That on the whole she won the day,
The fact is due to Sin.
The Fleet was hardly ten weeks out,

When somebody descried
The enemy. Sin gave a shout,
The Helmsmen put the ship about;
For, upon either side,
Tactics demanded a retreat.
Due west retired the foreign fleet,
But Sin he steered due east;
He muttered, 'They shall never meet.'
And when, towards the close of day,
The foemen were at least
Fifteen or twenty miles away,
He called his cabin-steward aft,
The boldest of his men;
He grasped him by the hand; he laughed
A fearless laugh, and then,
'Heaven help the right! Full steam a-head,
Fighting for fighting's sake,' he said.

Due west the foe – due east he steered.
Ah, me! the very stokers cheered,
And faces black with coal
And fuzzy with a five days' beard
Popped up, and yelled, and disappeared
Each in its little hole.
Long after they were out of sight,
Long after dark, throughout the night,
Throughout the following day,
He went on fighting all the time!
Not war, perhaps, but how sublime!

Just as he would have stepped ashore,
The President of Ecuador
Came on his quarter-deck;
Embraced him twenty times or more,

And gave him stripes and things galore,
Crosses and medals by the score,
And handed him a cheque –
And then a little speech he read.

Of twenty years, your sentence said,
That you should serve – another week
(Alas! it shames me as I speak)
Was owing when you quitted.
In recognition of your nerve,
It gives me pleasure to observe
The time you still had got to serve
Is totally remitted.

Instead of which these friends of mine' –
And here he pointed to a line
Of Colonels on the Quay –
'Have changed your sentence to a fine
Made payable to me.
No – do not thank me – not a word!
I am very glad to say
This little cheque is quite a third
Of what you have to pay.'

The crew they cheered and cheered again,
The simple loyal-hearted men!

Such deeds could never fail to be
Renowned throughout the west.
It was our cousins over sea
That loved the Sailor best, –
Our Anglo-Saxon kith and kin,
They doted on Commander Sin,
And gave him a tremendous feast
The week before we started.

O'Hooligan, and Vonderbeast,
And Nicolazzi, and the rest,
Were simply broken-hearted.

They came and ate and cried, 'God speed!'
The Bill was very large indeed,
And paid for by an Anglo-Saxon
Who bore the sterling name of Jackson.
On this occasion Sin was seen
Toasting McKinley and the Queen.
The speech was dull, but not an eye,
Not even the champagne, was dry.

III

Now William Blood, or, as I still
Affectionately call him, Bill,
Was of a different stamp;
One who, in other ages born,
Had turned to strengthen and adorn
The Senate or the Camp.
But Fortune, jealous and austere,
Had marked him for a great career
Of more congenial kind –
A sort of modern Buccaneer,
Commercial and refined.
Like all great men, his chief affairs
Were buying stocks and selling shares.
He occupied his mind
In buying them by day from men
Who needed ready cash, and then
At evening selling them again
To those with whom he dined.

But such a task could never fill
His masterful ambition.
That rapid glance, that iron will,
Disdained (and rightfully) to make
A profit here and there, or take
His two per cent commission.
His soul with nobler stuff was fraught;
The love of country, as it ought,
Haunted his every act and thought.
To that he lent his mighty powers,
To that he gave his waking hours,
Of that he dreamed in troubled sleep,
Till, after many years, the deep
    Imperial emotion,
That moves us like a martial strain,
Turned his Napoleonic brain
    To company promotion.

He failed, and it was better so:
    It made our expedition.
One day (it was a year ago)
He came on foot across the town,
And said his luck was rather down,
And would I lend him half-a-crown?
    I did, but on condition
(Drawn up in proper legal shape,
Witnessed and sealed, and tied with tape,
And costing two pound two)
That, 'If within the current year
He made a hundred thousand clear,'
He should accompany me in
A Project I had formed with Sin
    To go to Timbuctoo.
Later, we had a tiff because
I introduced another clause,

Of which the general sense is,
That Blood, in the unlikely case
Of this adventure taking place,
    Should pay the whole expenses.
Blood swore that he had never read
Or seen the clause. But Blood is dead.

Well, through a curious stroke of luck,
That very afternoon, he struck
    A new concern, in which,
By industry and honest ways,
He grew (to his eternal praise!)
In something less than sixty days
    Inordinately rich.

Let me describe what he became
    The day that he succeeded –
Though, in the searching light that Fame
Has cast on that immortal name,
    The task is hardly needed.

The world has very rarely seen
A deeper gulf than stood between
    The men who were my friends.
And, speaking frankly, I confess
They never cared to meet, unless
It served their private ends.

Sin loved the bottle, William gold;
'Twas Blood that bought and Sin that sold,
    In all their mutual dealings.
Blood never broke the penal laws;
Sin did it all the while, because
    He had the finer feelings.

Blood had his dreams, but Sin was mad:
While Sin was foolish, Blood was bad,
Sin, though I say it, was a cad.
      (And if the word arouses
Some criticism, pray reflect
How twisted was his intellect,
And what a past he had!)
But Blood was exquisitely bred,
      And always in the swim,
And people were extremely glad
      To ask him to their houses.
Be not too eager to condemn:
It was not he that hunted them,
      But they that hunted him.

In this fair world of culture made
For men of his peculiar trade,
Of all the many parts he played,
The part he grew to like the best
Was called 'the self-respecting guest.'
      And for that very reason
He found himself in great request
      At parties in the season,
Wherever gentlemen invest,
      From Chelsea to Mayfair.
From Lath and Stucco Gate, S.W.,
      To 90 Berkeley Square.
The little statesmen in the bud,
      The big provincial mayor,
      The man that owns a magazine,
      The authoress who might have been;
They always sent a card to Blood,
      And Blood was always there.
At every dinner, crush or rout,
A little whirlpool turned about

The form immovable and stout,
    That marked the Millionaire.
Sin (you remember) could not stay
In any club for half a day,
    When once his name was listed;
But Blood belonged to ninety-four,
And would have joined as many more
    Had any more existed.
Sin at a single game would lose
A little host of I.O.U.s,
And often took the oath absurd
To break the punters or his word
    Before it was completed.
Blood was another pair of shoes:
A man of iron, cold and hard,
He very rarely touched a card,
But when he did he cheated.
Again, the origin of Sin
    Was doubtful and obscure;
Whereas, the Captain's origin
    Was absolutely sure.

A document affirms that he
Was born in 1853
Upon a German ship at sea,
    Just off the Grand Canary.
And though the log is rather free
And written too compactly,
We know the weather to a T,
The longitude to a degree,
The latitude exactly,
    And every detail is the same;
    We even know his Mother's name.
As to his father's occupation,
Creed, colour, character or nation,

(On which the rumours vary);
He said himself concerning it,
With admirably caustic wit,
   'I think the Public would much rather
   Be sure of me than of my father.'

The contrast curiously keen
   Their characters could yield
Was most conspicuously seen
   Upon the Tented Field.
Was there by chance a native tribe
To cheat, cajole, corrupt, or bribe? –
In such conditions Sin would burn
   To plunge into the fray,
While Blood would run the whole concern
   From fifty miles away.

He had, wherever honours vain
Were weighed against material gain,
A judgment, practical and sane,
   Peculiarly his own.
In this connection let me quote
An interesting anecdote
   Not generally known.
Before he sailed he might have been
   (If he had thought it paid him)
A military man of note.
Her gracious Majesty the Queen
   Would certainly have made him,
In spite of his advancing years,
A Captain of the Volunteers.
A certain Person of the Sort
That has great influence at Court,
   Assured him it was so;

And said, 'It simply lies with you
To get this little matter through.
You pay a set of trifling fees
To me – at any time you please –'
Blood stopped him with a 'No!'
'This signal favour of the Queen's
Is very burdensome. It means
A smart Review (for all I know),
In which I am supposed to show
    Strategical ability:
And after that tremendous fights
And sleeping out on rainy nights,
And much responsibility.
Thank you: I have my own position,
I need no parchment or commission,
And every one who knows my name
Will call me "Captain" just the same.'
There was our leader in a phrase;
A man of strong decisive ways,
    But reticent[1] and grim.
Though not an Englishman, I own,
Perhaps it never will be known
    What England lost in him!

IV

The ship was dropping down the stream,
The Isle of Dogs was just abeam,
    And Sin and Blood and I
Saw Greenwich Hospital go past,
And gave a look – for them the last –
    Towards the London sky!

[1] This reticence, which some have called hypocrisy,
Was but the sign of nature's aristocracy.

Ah! nowhere have I ever seen
A sky so pure and so serene!

Did we at length, perhaps, regret
    Our strange adventurous lot?
And were our eyes a trifle wet
With tears that we repressed, and yet
    Which started blinding hot?
Perhaps – and yet, I do not know.
For when we came to go below,
    We cheerfully admitted
That though there was a smell of paint
(And though a very just complaint
Had to be lodged against the food),
The cabin furniture was good
    And comfortably fitted.
And even out beyond the Nore
We did not ask to go ashore.

To turn to more congenial topics,
    I said a little while ago
    The food was very much below
The standard needed to prepare
Explorers for the special fare
Which all authorities declare
    Is needful in the tropics.
A Frenchman sitting next to us
Rejected the asparagus;
The turtle soup was often cold,
The ices hot, the omelettes old,
The coffee worse than I can tell;
And Sin (who had a happy knack
Of rhyming rapidly and well
Like Cyrano de Bergerac)

Said '*Quant à moi, je n'aime pas
Du tout ce pâté de foie gras!*'
But this fastidious taste
Succeeded in a startling way;
At Dinner on the following day
    They gave us Bloater Paste.
Well – hearty Pioneers and rough
    Should not be over nice;
I think these lines are quite enough,
    And hope they will suffice
To make the Caterers observe
The kind of person whom they serve. –

.   .   .

And yet I really must complain
About the Company's Champagne!
    This most expensive kind of wine
In England is a matter
Of pride or habit when we dine
    (Presumably the latter).
Beneath an equatorial sky
You must consume it or you die;
And stern indomitable men
Have told me, time and time again,
'The nuisance of the tropics is
The sheer necessity of fizz.'
Consider then the carelessness –
The lack of polish and address,
    The villainy in short,
Of serving what explorers think
To be a necessary drink
In bottles holding something less
    Than one Imperial quart,
And costing quite a shilling more
Than many grocers charge ashore.

At sea the days go slipping past.
Monotonous from first to last –
A trip like any other one
In vessels going south. The sun
  Grew higher and more fiery.
We lay and drank, and swore, and played
At Trick-my-neighbour in the shade;
And you may guess how every sight,
However trivial or slight,
  Was noted in my diary.
I have it here – the usual things –
A serpent (not the sort with wings)
  Came rising from the sea:
In length (as far as we could guess)
A quarter of a mile or less.
The weather was extremely clear,
The creature dangerously near
  And plain as it could be.
It had a bifurcated tail,
And in its mouth it held a whale.
Just north, I find, of Cape de Verd
We caught a very curious bird
  With horns upon its head;
And – not, as one might well suppose,
Web-footed or with jointed toes –
  But having hoofs instead.
As no one present seemed to know
Its use or name, I let it go.

On June the 7th after dark
A young and very hungry shark
  Came climbing up the side.
It ate the Chaplain and the Mate –
But why these incidents relate?

The public must decide,
That nothing in the voyage out
Was worth their bothering about,
Until we saw the coast, which looks
Exactly as it does in books.

v

Oh! Africa, mysterious Land!
Surrounded by a lot of sand
    And full of grass and trees,
And elephants and Afrikanders,
And politics and Salamanders,
And Germans seeking to annoy,
And horrible rhinoceroi,
And native rum in little kegs,
And savages called Touaregs
    (A kind of Soudanese).
And tons of diamonds, and lots
Of nasty, dirty Hottentots,
And coolies coming from the East;
And serpents, seven yards long at least,
    And lions, that retain
Their vigour, appetites and rage
Intact to an extreme old age,
    And never lose their mane.
Far Land of Ophir! Mined for gold
By lordly Solomon of old,
Who sailing northward to Perim
Took all the gold away with him,
    And left a lot of holes;
Vacuities that bring despair
    To those confiding souls
Who find that they have bought a share

[181]

In marvellous horizons, where
The Desert terrible and bare
   Interminably rolls.

Great Island! Made to be the bane
Of Mr Joseph Chamberlain.
Peninsula! Whose smouldering fights
Keep Salisbury awake at nights;
And furnished for a year or so
Such sport to M. Hanotaux.

Vast Continent! Whose cumbrous shape
Runs from Bizerta to the Cape
(Bizerta on the northern shore,
Concerning which, the French, they swore
It never should be fortified,
Wherein that cheerful people lied).

Thou nest of Sultans full of guile,
Embracing Zanzibar the vile
And Egypt, watered by the Nile
(Egypt, which is, as I believe,
The property of the Khedive):
Containing in thy many states
Two independent potentates,
   And one I may not name.

Look carefully at number three,
Not independent quite, but he
Is more than what he used to be.
To thee, dear goal, so long deferred
Like old Æneas – in a word
   To Africa we came.

We beached upon a rising tide
At Sasstown on the western side;

And as we touched the strand
I thought – I may have been mistook –
I thought the earth in terror shook
    To feel its Conquerors land.

VI

In getting up our Caravan
We met a most obliging man,
The Lord Chief Justice of Liberia,
And Minister of the Interior;
Cain Abolition Beecher Boz,
Worked like a Nigger – which he was –
    And in a single day
Procured us Porters, Guides, and kit,
And would not take a sou for it
    Until we went away.[1]
We wondered how this fellow made
Himself so readily obeyed,
And why the natives were so meek;
Until by chance we heard him speak,
And then we clearly understood
How great a Power for Social Good
    The African can be.
He said with a determined air:
'You are not what your fathers were;
Liberians, you are Free!
Of course, if you refuse to go –'
And here he made a gesture.
He also gave us good advice
Concerning Labour and its Price.
'In dealing wid de Native Scum,

---

[1] But when we went away, we found
A deficit of several pound.

[183]

Yo' cannot pick an' choose;
Yo' hab to promise um a sum
Ob wages, paid in Cloth and Rum.
But, Lordy! that's a ruse!
Yo' get yo' well on de Adventure,
And change de wages to Indenture.'

We did the thing that he projected,
The Caravan grew disaffected,
    And Sin and I consulted;
Blood understood the Native mind,
He said: 'We must be firm but kind.'
    A Mutiny resulted.
I never shall forget the way
That Blood upon this awful day
Preserved us all from death.
He stood upon a little mound,
Cast his lethargic eyes around,
And said beneath his breath:
'Whatever happens we have got
The Maxim Gun, and they have not.'

He marked them in their rude advance,
He hushed their rebel cheers;
With one extremely vulgar glance
He broke the Mutineers.
(I have a picture in my book
Of how he quelled them with a look.)
We shot and hanged a few, and then
The rest became devoted men.
And here I wish to say a word
Upon the way my heart was stirred
    By those pathetic faces.
Surely our simple duty here
Is both imperative and clear;

While they support us, we should lend
Our every effort to defend,
And from a higher point of view
To give the full direction due
    To all the native races.
And I, throughout the expedition,
Insisted upon this position.

VII

Well, after that we toiled away
At drawing maps, and day by day
Blood made an accurate survey
    Of all that seemed to lend
A chance, no matter how remote,
Of letting our financier float
That triumph of Imagination,
'The Libyan Association.'
    In this the 'Negroes' friend,
Was much concerned to show the way
Of making Missionaries pay.

At night our leader and our friend
    Would deal in long discourses
Upon this meritorious end,
And how he would arrange it.
'The present way is an abuse
    Of Economic Forces;
They Preach, but they do not Produce.
Observe how I would change it.
I'd have the Missionary lent,
Upon a plot of land,
A sum at twenty-five per cent;
And (if I understand

[185]

The kind of people I should get)
An ever-present risk of debt
Would make them work like horses,
And form the spur, or motive spring,
In what I call "developing
      The Natural resources";
While people who subscribe will find
Profit and Piety combined.'

Imagine how the Mighty Scheme,
The Goal, the Vision, and the Dream,
Developed in his hands!
With such a purpose, such a mind
Could easily become inclined
To use the worst of lands!
Thus once we found him standing still,
Enraptured, on a rocky hill;
Beneath his feet there stank
A swamp immeasurably wide,
Wherein a kind of fœtid tide
Rose rhythmical and sank,
Brackish and pestilent with weeds
And absolutely useless reeds,
It lay; but nothing daunted
At seeing how it heaved and steamed
He stood triumphant, and he seemed
Like one possessed or haunted.

With arms that welcome and rejoice,
We heard him gasping, in a voice
By strong emotion rendered harsh:
'That Marsh – that Admirable Marsh!'
The Tears of Avarice that rise
In purely visionary eyes

Were rolling down his nose.
He was no longer Blood the Bold,
The Terror of his foes;
But Blood inflamed with greed of gold.

He saw us, and at once became
The Blood we knew, the very same
Whom we had loved so long.
He looked affectionately sly,
And said, 'Perhaps you wonder why
My feelings are so strong?
You only see a swamp, but I –
My friends, I will explain it.
I know some gentlemen in town
Will give me fifty thousand down,
Merely for leave to drain it.'

A little later on we found
A piece of gently rolling ground
That showed above the flat.
Such a protuberance or rise
As wearies European eyes.
To common men, like Sin and me,
The Eminence appeared to be
As purposeless as that.
Blood saw another meaning there,
He turned with a portentous glare,
And shouted for the Native Name.
The Black interpreter in shame
Replied: 'The native name I fear
Is something signifying Mud.'
    Then, with the gay bravado
That suits your jolly Pioneer,

In his prospectus Captain Blood
    Baptized it 'Eldorado'.
He also said the Summit rose
Majestic with Eternal Snows.

VIII

Now it behoves me (or behooves
To give a retrospect that proves
    What foresight can achieve,
The kind of thing that (by the way)
Men in our cold agnostic day
Must come from Africa to say,
    From England to believe.

Blood had, while yet we were in town,
Said with his intellectual frown:
'Suppose a Rhino knocks you down
And walks upon you like a mat,
Think of the public irritation.
If with an incident like that,
We cannot give an illustration.'
Seeing we should be at a loss
To reproduce the scene,
We bought a stuffed rhinoceros,
A Kodak, and a screen.
We fixed a picture. William pressed
A button, and I did the rest.

To those Carnivora that make
An ordinary Person quake
    We did not give a care.
The Lion never will attack

A White, if he can get a Black.
And there were such a lot of these
We could afford with perfect ease
    To spare one here and there.
It made us more compact – and then –
It's right to spare one's fellow men.

Of far more consequence to us,
And much more worthy to detain us,
    The very creature that we feared
(I mean the white Rhinoceros,
'*Siste Viator Africanus*')
    In all its majesty appeared.

This large but peevish pachyderm
(To use a scientific term),
Though commonly herbivorous,
Is eminently dangerous.
It may be just the creature's play;
But people who have felt it say
That when he prods you with his horn
You wish you never had been born.

As I was dozing in the sun,
Without a cartridge to my gun,
    Upon a sultry day,
Absorbed in somnolescent bliss,
Just such an animal as this
    Came charging where I lay.
My only refuge was to fly.
But flight is not for me![1]
Blood happened to be standing by,

[1] Besides, I found my foot was caught
In twisted roots that held it taut.

He darted up a tree
And shouted, 'Do your best to try
And fix him with the Human Eye.'

Between a person and a beast
(But for the Human Eye at least)
The issue must be clear.
The tension of my nerves increased,
And yet I felt no fear.
Nay, do not praise me – not at all –
Courage is merely physical,
And several people I could name
Would probably have done the same.

I kept my glance extremely firm,
I saw the wretched creature squirm;
A look of terror over-spread
Its features, and it dropped down dead.
At least, I thought it did,
And foolishly withdrew my gaze,
When (finding it was rid
Of those mysterious piercing rays)
      It came to life again.
It jumped into the air, and came
With all its might upon my frame.

(Observe the posture of the hoof.
The wire and black support that look
So artificial in the proof
Will be deleted in the book.)

It did it thirty separate times;
When, luckily for all these rhymes,

Blood shot the brute – that is to say,
Blood shot, and then it ran away.

IX

We journeyed on in single file;
The march proceeded mile on mile
    Monotonous and lonely,
We saw (if I remember right)
The friendly features of a white
    On two occasions only.
The first was when our expedition
Came suddenly on a commission,
    Appointed to determine
Whether the thirteenth parallel
Ran right across a certain well,
Or touched a closely neighbouring tree;
And whether elephants should be
Exterminated all as 'game',
Or, what is not at all the same,
    Destroyed as common vermin.

To this commission had been sent
Great bigwigs from the Continent,
    And on the English side
Men of such ancient pedigree
As filled the soul of Blood with glee;
    He started up and cried:
'I'll go to them at once, and make
These young adventurous spirits take
    A proof of my desire
To use in this concern of ours
Their unsuspected business powers.
The bearers of historic names

[191]

Shall rise to something higher
Than haggling over frontier claims,
    And they shall find their last estate
    Enshrined in my directorate.'

In twenty minutes he returned,
His face with righteous anger burned,
And when we asked him what he'd done,
    He answered, 'They reject us,
I couldn't get a single one
    To come on the prospectus.
Their leader (though he was a Lord)
Stoutly refused to join the board,
And made a silly foreign speech
Which sounded like No Bless Ableech.
I'm used to many kinds of men,
And bore it very well; but, when
    It came to being twitted
On my historic Sporting Shirt,
I own I felt a trifle hurt;
    I took my leave and quitted.'

There is another side to this;
With no desire to prejudice
    The version of our leader,
I think I ought to drop a hint
Of what I shall be bound to print,
    In justice to the reader.
I followed, keeping out of sight;
And took in this ingenious way
A sketch that throws a certain light
On why the master went away.
No doubt he felt a trifle hurt,
It even may be true to say

They twitted him upon his shirt,
But isn't it a trifle thick
To talk of twitting with a stick?
Well, let it pass. He acted well.
This species of official swell,
  Especially the peer,
Who stoops to a delimitation
With any European nation
  Is doomed to disappear.
Blood said, 'They pass into the night.'
And men like Blood are always right.

The Second shows the full effect
Of ministerial neglect;
Sin, walking out alone in quest
Of Boa-constrictors that infest
  The Lagos Hinterland,
Got separated from the rest,
  And ran against a band
Of native soldiers led by three –
A Frenchman, an official Prussian,
And what we took to be a Russian –
  The very coalition
Who threaten England's power at sea,
And, but for men like Blood and me,
Would drive her navies from the sea,
  And hurl her to perdition.
But did my comrade think to flee?
To use his very words – Not he!
He turned with a contemptuous laugh.
Observe him in the photograph.
But still these bureaucrats pursued,
Until they reached the Captain's tent.
They grew astonishingly rude;
The Russian simply insolent,

Announcing that he had been sent
    Upon a holy mission,
To call for the disarmament
    Of all our expedition.
He said 'the miseries of war
Had touched his master to the core';
    It was extremely vexing
To hear him add, 'he couldn't stand
This passion for absorbing land;
    He hoped we weren't annexing.'
The German asked with some brutality
To have our names and nationality.
    I had an inspiration,
In words methodical and slow
I gave him this decisive blow:
    'I haven't got a nation.'
Perhaps the dodge was rather low,
And yet I wasn't wrong to
Escape the consequences so;
For, on my soul, I did not know
What nation to belong to.

The German gave a searching look,
And marked me in his little book:
'The features are a trifle Dutch –
    Perhaps he is a Fenian;
He may be a Maltese, but much
    More probably Armenian.'

Blood gave us each a trifling sum
To say that he was deaf and dumb,
    And backed the affirmation
By gestures so extremely rum,
They marked him on the writing pad:

[194]

'Not only deaf and dumb, but mad.'
    It saved the situation.
'If such a man as *that*' (said they)
'Is Leader, they can go their way.'

X

Thus, greatly to our ease of mind,
Our foreign foes we left behind;
But dangers even greater
Were menacing our path instead.
In every book I ever read
Of travels on the Equator,
A plague, mysterious and dread,
Imperils the narrator;
He always very nearly dies,
But doesn't, which is calm and wise.
Said Sin, the indolent and vague,
'D'you think that we shall get the plague?'
It followed tragically soon;
In fording an immense lagoon,
We let our feet get damp.
Next morning I began to sneeze,
The awful enemy, Disease,
Had fallen on the camp!
With Blood the malady would take
An allotropic form
Of intermittent stomach ache,
While Sin grew over warm;
Complained of weakness in the knees,
An inability to think,
A strong desire to dose and drink,
    And lie upon his back.

For many a long delirious day,
Each in his individual way
    Succumbed to the attack.

XI

Our litters lay upon the ground
With heavy curtains shaded round;
    The Plague had passed away.
We could not hear a single sound,
    And wondered as we lay –
'Perhaps the Forest Belt is passed,
And Timbuctoo is reached at last,
The while our faithful porters keep
So still to let their masters sleep.'

Poor Blood and I were far too weak
To raise ourselves, or even speak;
    We lay, content to languish.
When Sin, to make the matter certain,
Put out his head beyond the curtain.
    And cried in utter anguish:
'This is not Timbuctoo at all,
But just a native Kraal or Crawl;
And, what is more, our Caravan
Has all deserted to a man.'

        .   .   .

At evening they returned to bring
Us prisoners to their savage king,
    Who seemed upon the whole
A man urbane and well inclined;
He said, 'You shall not be confined,
    But left upon parole.'

[196]

Blood, when he found us both alone,
Lectured in a pedantic tone,
    And yet with quaint perfection,
On 'Prisons Systems I have known.'
    He said in this connection:

'The primal process is to lug
A Johnny to the cells – or jug.
Dear Henry will not think me rude,
If – just in passing – I allude
To Quod or Penal Servitude.
Of every form, Parole I take
To be the easiest to break.'

On hearing this we ran
To get the guns, and then we laid
An admirable ambuscade,
In which to catch our man.
We hid behind a little knoll,
    And waited for our prey
To take his usual morning stroll
    Along the fatal way.
All unsuspecting and alone
He came into the danger zone,
    The range of which we knew
To be one furlong and a third,
And then – an incident occurred
Which, I will pledge my sacred word,
    Is absolutely true.

Blood took a very careful aim,
And Sin and I did just the same;
Yet by some strange and potent charm
The King received no kind of harm!

He wore, as it appears,
A little fetich on a thread,
A mumbo-jumbo, painted red,
Gross and repulsive in the head,
    Especially the ears.

Last year I should have laughed at it,
But now with reverence I admit
That nothing in the world is commoner
Than Andrew Lang's Occult Phenomena.

On getting back to England, I
Described the matter to the Psy-
    Chological Committee.

Of course they thanked me very much;
But said, 'We have a thousand such,
    And it would be a pity.
To break our standing resolution,
And pay for any contribution.'

XII

The King was terribly put out;
To hear him call the guard and shout,
    And stamp, and curse, and rave
Was (as the Missionaries say)
A lesson in the Godless way
The heathen will behave.
He sent us to a prison, made
Of pointed stakes in palisade,
    And there for several hours
Our Leader was a mark for bricks,
And eggs and coconuts and sticks,

And pussy-cats in showers.
Our former porters seemed to bear
A grudge against the millionaire.

And yet the thing I minded most
    Was not the ceaseless teasing
(With which the Captain was engrossed),
Nor being fastened to a post
(Though that was far from pleasing);
But hearing them remark that they
'Looked forward to the following day.'

XIII

At length, when we were left alone,
Sin twisted with a hollow groan,
    And bade the Master save
His comrades by some bold device,
    From the impending grave.

Said Blood: 'I never take advice,
But every man has got his price;
We must maintain the open door
Yes, even at the cost of war!'
    He shifted his position,
And drafted in a little while
A note in diplomatic style
    Containing a condition.

'If them that wishes to be told
As how there is a bag of gold,
    And where a party hid it;
Mayhap as other parties knows
A thing or two, and there be those

As seen the man wot hid it.'
The Monarch read it through, and wrote
A little sentence most emphatical:
'I think the language of the note
Is strictly speaking not grammatical.'
On seeing our acute distress,
The King – I really must confess –
    Behaved uncommon handsome;
He said he would release the three
If only Captain Blood and he
    Could settle on a ransom.
And it would clear the situation
To hear his private valuation.

'My value,' William Blood began,
'Is ludicrously small.
I think I am the vilest man
That treads this earthly ball;
My head is weak, my heart is cold,
I'm ugly, vicious, vulgar, old,
Unhealthy, short and fat.
I cannot speak, I cannot work,
I have the temper of a Turk,
    And cowardly at that.
Retaining, with your kind permission,
The usual five per cent commission,
I think that I could do the job
For seventeen or sixteen bob.'

The King was irritated, frowned,
And cut him short with, 'Goodness Gracious!
Your economics are fallacious!
I quite believe you are a wretch,
But things are worth what they will fetch.

I'll put your price at something round,
Say, six-and-thirty thousand pound?'
But just as Blood began with zest
To bargain, argue, and protest,
  Commander Sin and I
Broke in: 'Your Majesty was told
About a certain bag of gold;
  If you will let us try,
We'll find the treasure, for we know
The place to half a yard or so.'

Poor William! The suspense and pain
Had touched the fibre of his brain;
  So far from showing gratitude,
He cried in his delirium: 'Oh!
For Heaven's sake don't let them go.'
  Only a lunatic would take
   So singular an attitude,
  When loyal comrades for his sake
  Had put their very lives at stake.

   .   .   .

The King was perfectly content
To let us find it – and we went.
But as we left we heard him say,
  'If there is half an hour's delay
  The Captain will have passed away.'

XIV

Alas! within a single week
The Messengers despatched to seek
  Our hiding-place had found us,
We made an excellent defence
(I use the word in legal sense),

[201]

But none the less they bound us.
(Not in the legal sense at all
But with a heavy chain and ball).
With barbarism past belief
They flaunted in our faces
The relics of our noble chief;
With insolent grimaces,
Raised the historic shirt before
Our eyes, and pointed on the floor
To dog-eared cards and loaded dice,
It seems they sold him by the slice.
Well, every man has got his price.

The horrors followed thick and fast,
I turned my head to give a last
Farewell to Sin; but, ah! too late,
I only saw his horrid fate –
Some savages around a pot
That seemed uncomfortably hot;
And in the centre of the group
My dear companion making soup.

Then I was pleased to recognize
Two thumbscrews suited to my size,
And I was very glad to see
That they were going to torture me.
I find that torture pays me best,
It simply teems with interest.

They hung me up above the floor
Head downwards by a rope;
They thrashed me half an hour or more,
They filled my mouth with soap;
They jabbed me with a pointed pole

To make me lose my self-control,
    But they did not succeed.
Till (if it's not too coarse to state)
There happened what I simply hate,
    My nose began to bleed.
Then, I admit, I said a word
Which luckily they never heard;
But in a very little while
My calm and my contemptuous smile
    Compelled them to proceed.
They filed my canine teeth to points
    And made me bite my tongue.
They racked me till they burst my joints,
    And after that they hung
A stone upon my neck that weighed
At least a hundred pounds, and made
Me run like mad for twenty miles,
And climb a lot of lofty stiles.
They tried a dodge that rarely fails,
The tub of Regulus with nails –
The cask is rather rude and flat,
But native casks are all like that –
The nails stuck in for quite an inch,
But did I flinch? I did not flinch.
In tones determined, loud, and strong
I sang a patriotic song,
Thank Heaven it did not last for long!
    My misery was past;
My superhuman courage rose
Superior to my savage foes;
    They worshipped me at last.
With many heartfelt compliments,
They sent me back at their expense,
And here I am returned to find
The pleasures I had left behind.

To go the London rounds!
To note the quite peculiar air
Of courtesy, and everywhere
The same unfailing public trust
In manuscript that fetches just
A thousand! not of thin Rupees,
Nor Reis (which are Portuguese),
Nor Rubles; but a thousand clear
Of heavy, round, impressive, dear,
Familiar English pounds!

Oh! England, who would leave thy shores –
Excuse me, but I see it bores
A busy journalist
To hear a rhapsody which he
Could write without detaining me,
So I will not insist.
Only permit me once again
    To make it clearly understood
That both those honourable men,
    Commander Sin and Captain Blood,
Would swear to all that I have said,
Were they alive;
    but they are dead!

IMITATION

Hen: – Therefore do thou, stiff-set Northumberland,
    Retire to Chester, and my cousin here,
    The noble Bedford, hie to Glo'ster straight
    And give our Royal ordinance and word
    That in this fit and strife of empery
    No loss shall stand account. To this compulsion

I pledge my sword, my person and my honour
On the Great Seal of England: so farewell.
Swift to your charges: nought was ever done
Unless at some time it were first begun.

LORD LUNDY

WHO WAS TOO FREELY MOVED TO TEARS,
AND THEREBY RUINED HIS
POLITICAL CAREER

Lord Lundy from his earliest years
Was far too freely moved to Tears.
For instance, if his Mother said,
'Lundy! It's time to go to Bed!'
He bellowed like a Little Turk.
Or if his father, Lord Dunquerque,
Said, 'Hi!' in a Commanding Tone,
'Hi, Lundy! Leave the Cat alone!'
Lord Lundy, letting go its tail,
Would raise so terrible a wail
As moved his Grandpapa the Duke
To utter the severe rebuke:
'When I, Sir! was a little Boy,
An Animal was not a Toy!'

His father's Elder Sister, who
Was married to a Parvenoo,
Confided to Her Husband, 'Drat!
The Miserable, Peevish Brat!
Why don't they drown the Little Beast?'
Suggestions which, to say the least,

Are not what we expect to hear
From Daughters of an English Peer.
His grandmamma, His Mother's Mother,
Who had some dignity or other,
The Garter, or no matter what,
I can't remember all the Lot!
Said, 'Oh! that I were Brisk and Spry
To give him that for which to cry!'
(An empty wish, alas! for she
Was Blind and nearly ninety-three).

The Dear old Butler thought – but there!
I really neither know nor care
For what the Dear Old Butler thought!
In my opinion, Butlers ought
To know their place, and not to play
The Old Retainer night and day.
I'm getting tired and so are you,
Let's cut the Poem into two!

.   .   .

LORD LUNDY

(*Second Canto*)

It happened to Lord Lundy then,
As happens to so many men:
Towards the age of twenty-six,
They shoved him into politics;
In which profession he commanded
The income that his rank demanded
In turn as Secretary for
India, the Colonies, and War.
But very soon his friends began
To doubt if he were quite the man:

Thus, if a member rose to say
(As members do from day to day),
'Arising out of that reply . . .!'
Lord Lundy would begin to cry.
A Hint at harmless little jobs
Would shake him with convulsive sobs.

While as for Revelations, these
Would simply bring him to his knees,
And leave him whimpering like a child.
It drove his Colleagues raving wild!
They let him sink from Post to Post,
From fifteen hundred at the most
To eight, and barely six – and then
To be Curator of Big Ben! . . .
And finally there came a Threat
To oust him from the Cabinet!

The Duke – his aged grand-sire – bore
The shame till he could bear no more.
He rallied his declining powers,
Summoned the youth to Brackley Towers,
And bitterly addressed him thus –
'Sir! you have disappointed us!
We had intended you to be
The next Prime Minister but three:
The stocks were sold; the Press was squared;
The Middle Class was quite prepared.
But as it is! . . . My language fails!
Go out and govern New South Wales!'

.   .   .

The Aged Patriot groaned and died:
And gracious! how Lord Lundy cried!

During a late election Lord
Roehampton strained a vocal chord
From shouting, very loud and high,
To lots and lots of people why
The Budget in his own opin-
-Ion should not be allowed to win.
He sought a Specialist, who said:
'You have a swelling in the head:
Your Larynx is a thought relaxed
And you are greatly over-taxed.'
'I am indeed! On every side!'
The Earl (for such he was) replied
In hoarse excitement . . . 'Oh! My Lord,
You jeopardize your vocal chord!'
Broke in the worthy Specialist.
'Come! Here's the treatment! I insist!
To Bed! to Bed! And do not speak
A single word till Wednesday week,
When I will come and set you free
(If you are cured) and take my fee.'
On Wednesday week the Doctor hires
A Brand-new Car with Brand-new Tyres
And Brand-new Chauffeur all complete
For visiting South Audley Street.

.   .   .

But what is this? No Union Jack
Floats on the Stables at the back!
No Toffs escorting Ladies fair
Perambulate the Gay Parterre.
A 'Scutcheon hanging lozenge-wise
And draped in crape appals his eyes
Upon the mansion's ample door,

To which he wades through heaps of Straw,[1]
And which a Butler, drowned in tears,
On opening but confirms his fears:
'Oh! Sir! – Prepare to hear the worst! . . .
Last night my kind old master burst.
And what is more, I doubt if he
Has left enough to pay your fee.
The Budget – ' With a dreadful oath,
The Specialist, denouncing both
The Budget *and* the House of Lords,
Buzzed angrily Bayswaterwards.

. . .

And ever since, as I am told,
Gets it beforehand; and in gold.

LORD CALVIN

Lord Calvin thought the Bishops should not sit
As Peers of Parliament. And *argued* it!
In spite of which, for years, and years, and years,
They went on sitting with their fellow-peers.

LORD HENRY CHASE

What happened to Lord Henry Chase?
He got into a Libel Case!
The Daily Howl had said that he –
But could not prove it perfectly
To Judge or Jury's satisfaction:
His Lordship, therefore, won the action.
But, as the damages were small,
He gave them to a Hospital.

[1] This is the first and only time
That I have used this sort of Rhyme.

LORD HEYGATE

Lord Heygate had a troubled face,
His furniture was commonplace –
The sort of Peer who well might pass
For someone of the middle class.
I do not think you want to hear
About this unimportant Peer,
So let us leave him to discourse
About Lord Epsom and his horse.

LORD EPSOM

A Horse Lord Epsom did bestride
With mastery and quiet pride.
He dug his spurs into its hide.
The Horse, discerning it was pricked,
Incontinently bucked and kicked,
A thing that no one could predict!

Lord Epsom clearly understood
The High-bred creature's nervous mood,
As only such a horseman could.
Dismounting, he was heard to say
That it was kinder to delay
His pleasure to a future day.

.   .   .

He had the Hunter led away.

LORD FINCHLEY

Lord Finchley tried to mend the Electric Light
Himself. It struck him dead: And serve him right!
It is the business of the wealthy man
To give employment to the artisan.

LORD ALI-BABA

Lord Ali-Baba was a Turk
Who hated every kind of work,
And would repose for hours at ease
With Houris seated on his knees.
A happy life! – Until, one day
Mossoo Alphonse Effendi Bey
(A Younger Turk: the very cream
And essence of the New Régime)
Dispelled this Oriental dream
By granting him a place at Court,
High Coffee-grinder to the Porte,
Unpaid: – In which exalted Post
His Lordship yielded up the ghost.

LORD HIPPO

Lord Hippo suffered fearful loss
By putting money on a horse
Which he believed, if it were pressed,
Would run far faster than the rest:
For someone who was in the know
Had confidently told him so.
But on the morning of the race
It only took the *seventh* place!
Picture the Viscount's great surprise!
He scarcely could believe his eyes!
He sought the Individual who
Had laid him odds at 9 to 2,
Suggesting as a useful tip
That they should enter Partnership
And put to joint account the debt
Arising from his foolish bet.

But when the Bookie – oh! my word,
I only wish you could have heard
The way he roared he did not think,
And hoped that they might strike him pink!
Lord Hippo simply turned and ran
From this infuriated man.
Despairing, maddened and distraught
He utterly collapsed and sought
His sire, the Earl of Potamus,
And brokenly addressed him thus:
'Dread Sire – to-day – at Ascot – I . . .'
His genial parent made reply:
'Come! Come! Come! Come! Don't look so glum!
Trust your Papa and name the sum . . .
What? . . . Fifteen hundred thousand? . . . Hum!
However . . . stiffen up, you wreck;
Boys will be boys – so here's the cheque!'
Lord Hippo, feeling deeply – well,
More grateful than he cared to tell –
Punted the lot on Little Nell: –
And got a telegram at dinner
To say that he had backed the Winner!

LORD UNCLE TOM

Lord Uncle Tom was different from
    What other nobles are.
For they are yellow or pink, I think,
    But he was black as tar.

He had his Father's debonair
    And rather easy pride:
But his complexion and his hair
    Were from the mother's side.

He often mingled in debate
　　And latterly displayed
Experience of peculiar weight
　　Upon the Cocoa-trade.

But now he speaks no more. The *Bill*
　　Which he could not abide,
It preyed upon his mind until
　　He sickened, paled, and died.

LORD LUCKY

Lord Lucky, by a curious fluke,
Became a most important duke.
From living in a vile Hotel
A long way east of Camberwell
He rose, in less than half an hour,
To riches, dignity and power.
It happened in the following way: –
The Real Duke went out one day
To shoot with several people, one
Of whom had never used a gun.
This gentleman (a Mr Meyer
Of Rabley Abbey, Rutlandshire),
As he was scrambling through the brake,
Discharged his weapon by mistake,
And plugged about an ounce of lead
Piff-bang into his Grace's Head –
Who naturally fell down dead.
His Heir, Lord Ugly, roared, 'You Brute!
Take that to teach you how to shoot!'
Whereat he volleyed, left and right;
But being somewhat short of sight,
His right-hand Barrel only got

The second heir, Lord Poddleplot;
The while the left-hand charge (or choke)
Accounted for another bloke,
Who stood with an astounded air
Bewildered by the whole affair
– And was the third remaining heir.
After the Execution (which
Is something rare among the Rich)
Lord Lucky, while of course he needed
Some help to prove his claim, succeeded.
– But after his succession, though
All this was over years ago,
He only once indulged the whim
Of asking Meyer to lunch with him.

LORD CANTON

The reason that the present Lord Canton
Succeeded lately to his Brother John
Was that his Brother John, the elder son,
Died rather suddenly at forty-one.
The insolence of an Italian guide
Appears to be the reason that he died.

LORD ABBOTT

Lord Abbott's coronet was far too small,
So small, that as he sauntered down Whitehall
Even the youthful Proletariat
(Who probably mistook if for a Hat)
Remarked on its exiguous extent.
There is a picture of the incident.

ANOTHER PEER

Lord Archibald I grieve to say
Was late for breakfast every day,
And as he slunk upon the scene
His kind papa – a Rural Dean –
Would solemnly remark 'My son
Our morning meal is nearly done
And grace will very soon be said.'
Lord Archibald would hang his head
And drop hot tears upon his plate:
And yet next morning would be late.

LORD RUMBO AND LORD JUMBO

Lord Rumbo was a Democrat
Who wore a very curious hat
And woollen boots, and didn't think
It right to smoke or take a drink.

He also thought it rather wrong
To hum the chorus of a song.
But what he simply couldn't stand
Was Billiard Tables off the Strand.

Yes! Billiard Tables off the Strand!
Lord Jumbo, on the other hand,
Was quite another sort of cove.
What? Yes by God! – and also Jove.

He was a Tory thick and thin.
His hat was made of Beaver Skin.
He practised every kind of sport
And drank a dreadful deal of Port.

Hail Muse. Inspire your devotee
– Which is on this occasion me –
With power to tell in phrase refined
The end of Joseph Nevermind:
With power to tell his glorious end
Without one word which could offend.
For twenty years – or rather more –
This – shall I say this ghastly bore? –
Had held the seat of Smoke-on-Tees
With varying majorities; –
But always held it – mark you that!
I would not call his wife a cat,
But she was sexless, rich and sour,
Three things which greatly serve the power
Of ladies in constituencies:
Particularly, Smoke-on-Tees.
These two, this couple, nay this pair,
Had got so tight a cinch up there
As kept unstained through every fight
The glorious name of Oomptyite,
And Oomptyism could not find
A stronger name than Nevermind.
They (I discreetly call them 'they'
– It is the least that I could say –)
Were tempted in the end by fate
To make him Minister of State,
In which capacity he showed
The mental vigour of a toad,
The all-round grasp of things and men
Which flourishes beneath Big Ben;
A power of work observed in both
The lap-dog and the common sloth,
And finally that concentration

And faculty for integration
So common in his social station.
 They' therefore laid him on the shelf
(If I may so express myself),
Whereat what – well, what I suppose
A gentleman might call his *nose*
Was – not to put too fine a point
Upon the matter – out of joint,
And yet he had a great reward!
A youth whose Uncle was a lord
(A *real* lord you understand)
Became his secretary and
His debtor and a lot beside.
So when he died – why, when he *died*
The papers loaded him with praise . . .
In some respects: in several ways.

TO A LITTLE MAN IN PALL MALL

Ho! Little man with hat askew
And cigarette in mouth – to *you*
To you with drooping cigarette
And drooping eyelids, and with yet
That movement as of something not
Quite lost in all our modern rot,
Some hope, some humour, and some fire
I touch – and only touch – my lyre.

Do you consent that all we did
From Ganges to the Pyramid;
From Hercules his pillars high
That mountainously guard the sky
To the new lands: to all that East
Which Drake unto the very least
Of seamen gloried to behold

And minted it in English gold,
– In gold much greater than mere gold,
Gold of the fighters and good gold –
Do you consent that we shall fall
To be the vilest of them all,
The vilest of the modern herd,
Gagged, poisoned, ridiculed, absurd?
A prey to usurers and knaves,
First dupes, then cowards, lastly slaves?
Boasting – but not to fight the strong;
Armoured (against our will) for wrong,
And beaten in some last small fight,
Because we blinkered at the light?

Do you desire to see my land,
Which you and I so understand,
Beloved England, for her sins,
Pushed back to bestial origins?
Made abject, voiding pride, and then
A market where they purchase men;
A stews, a pawnshop, a buffoon?
You don't? Then wake extremely soon
And do some sweeping. Sweep away
The mess that blocks your door to-day.
Sweep all the foulness off you. Strip
The clothes that baulk your fellowship.
Remember manhood. Take the chance
Of firing lines in their advance.
Mark the tall figures of the foe,
And risk a bullet, lad! But no,
You won't adventure? Very well.
Go down, with all you are, to Hell,
And suffer – Person in Pall Mall.

The Rich arrived in pairs
And also in Rolls Royces;
They talked of their affairs
In loud and strident voices.

(The Husbands and the Wives
Of this select society
Lead independent lives
Of infinite variety.)

The Poor arrived in Fords,
Whose features they resembled;
They laughed to see so many Lords
And Ladies all assembled.

The People in Between
Looked underdone and harassed
And out of place and mean,
And horribly embarrassed.

For the hoary social curse
Gets hoarier and hoarier,
And it stinks a trifle worse
Than in the days of Queen Victoria,
When they married and gave in marriage,
They danced at the County Ball,
And some of them kept a carriage.
And the flood destroyed them all.

WILLIAM SHAND

There was a man called William Shand,
He had the habit of command,

And when subordinates would shout
He used to bang them all about.
It happened, by a turn of Fate,
Himself became sub-ordinate,
Through being passenger upon
A liner, going to Ceylon.
One day, as they were in the Red
(Or Libyan) Sea, the Captain said:
'I think it's coming on to blow.
Let everybody go below!'
But William Shand said: 'Not for me.
I'm going to stop on deck!' said he.
The Captain, wounded in his pride,
Summoned the Second Mate aside
And whispered: 'Surely Mr Shand
Must be extremely rich by land?'
'No,' said the Mate, 'when last ashore
I watched him. He is rather poor.'
'Ho!' cried the Captain. 'Stands it thus?
And shall the knave make mock of us?
I'll teach him to respect his betters.
Here, Bo'swain! Put the man in fetters!'
In fetters therefore William lay
Until the liner reached Bombay,
When he was handed to the court
Which deals with cases of the sort
In that uncomfortable port;
Which promptly hanged him out of hand.
Such was the fate of William Shand.

Moral
The moral is that people must,
If they are poor, obey or bust.

THE THREE RACES

Behold, my child, the Nordic Man
And be as like him as you can.
His legs are long; his mind is slow;
His hair is lank and made of tow.

And here we have the Alpine Race.
Oh! What a broad and foolish face!
His skin is of a dirty yellow,
He is a most unpleasant fellow.

The most degraded of them all
Mediterranean we call;
His hair is crisp, and even curls,
And he is saucy with the girls.

OBITER DICTA

I

SIR HENRY WAFFLE K.C. (*continuing*)

Sir Anthony Habberton, Justice and Knight,
Was enfeoffed of two acres of land
And it doesn't sound much till you hear that the site
Was a strip to the South of the Strand.

HIS LORDSHIP (*Obiter Dictum*)

A strip to the South of the Strand
Is a good situation for land.
It is healthy and dry
And sufficiently high
And convenient on every hand.

[221]

II

SIR HENRY WAFFLE K.C. (*continuing*)
Now Sir Anthony, shooting in Timberley Wood,
Was imprudent enough to take cold;
And he died without warning at six in the morning,
Because he was awfully old.

HIS LORDSHIP (*Obiter Dictum*)
I have often been credibly told
That when people are awfully old
Though cigars are a curse
And strong waters are worse
There is nothing so fatal as cold.

III

SIR HENRY WAFFLE K.C. (*continuing*)
But Archibald answered on hearing the news:
'I never move out till I must'.
Which was all very jolly for *Cestui que Use*
But the Devil for *Cestui que Trust*.

HIS LORDSHIP (*Obiter Dictum*)
The office of *Cestui que Trust*
Is reserved for the learned and just.
Any villain you choose
May be *Cestui que Use*,
But a Lawyer for Cestui que Trust.

IV

SIR HENRY WAFFLE K.C. (*continuing*)
Now the ruling laid down in *Regina v. Brown*
May be cited . . .

HIS LORDSHIP (*rising energetically*)
You're wrong! It may not!
I've strained all my powers
For some thirty-six hours
To unravel this pestilent rot.

THE WHOLE COURT (*rising and singing in chorus*)
Your Lordship is sound to the core.
It is nearly a quarter to four.
We've had quite enough of this horrible stuff
And we don't want to hear any more!

LITTLE SILLY MAN (*rising at the back of the Court*)
Your Lordship is perfectly right.
He can't go on rhyming all night.
I suggest . . .
   (*He is gagged, bound and dragged off to a Dungeon*).

THE STATESMAN

I knew a man whose used to say,
Not once but twenty times a day,
That in the turmoil and the strife
(His very words) of Public Life
The thing of ultimate effect
Was Character – not Intellect.
He therefore was at strenuous pains
To atrophy his puny brains
And registered success in this
Beyond the dreams of avarice,
Till, when he had at last become
Blind, paralytic, deaf and dumb,
Insensible and cretinous,
He was admitted ONE OF US.

[223]

They therefore, (meaning Them by 'They')
His colleagues of the N.C.A.,
The T.U.C., the I.L.P.,
Appointed him triumphantly
To bleed the taxes of a clear
200,000 Francs a year
(Swiss), as the necessary man
For Conferences at Lausanne,
Geneva, Basle, Locarno, Berne:
A salary which he will earn,
Yes – *earn* I say – until he Pops,
Croaks, passes in his checks and Stops: –
When he will be remembered for
A week, a month, or even more.

THE AUTHOR

There is a literary man,
Whose name is Herbert Keanes:
His coat is lined with astrakhan.
He lives on private means.

His house is in St James's Square
(Which I could not afford).
His head is strong but short of hair,
His Uncle is a Lord.

This Uncle loves him like a son
And has been heard to vow
He will be famous later on
And even might be now.

And he has left him in his will
New Boyton, Hatton Strand,
Long Stokely, Pilly-on-the-Hill,
And Lower Sandiland.

[224]

He is not dead, but when he dies
This wealth will all accrue,
Unless the old gafoozler lies,
O Herbert Keanes, to you!

The Son? The Son whom *She* alone
Could bear to such a sire,
The son of Lady Jane O'Hone
And Henry Keanes Esquire.

First with a private tutor, then
At Eton Herbert Keanes,
Like other strong successful men,
Was nurtured in his teens.

To curious dons he next would pay
His trifling entrance fee,
And was accepted, strange to say,
By those of Trinity:

Tall Trinity whereby the Cam
Its awful torrent rolls,
But there! – I do not care a damn,
It might have been All Souls.

Has sat for Putticombe in Kent
But lost the seat he won
By boldly saying what he meant
Though meaning he had none.

Has written 'Problems of the Poor,'
'The Future of Japan'
And 'Musings by Killarney's Shore'
And 'What Indeed is Man?'

And 'Flowers and Fruit' (a book of verse)
'The Ethics of St Paul,'
'Was there a Peter?' (rather worse)
And 'Nero' (worst of all).

Clubs: Handy Dandy, Beagle's, Tree's,
Pitt, Palmerston, Riviere,
The Walnut Box, Empedocles,
Throgmorton, Pot o' Beer.

(The last for its bohemian lists
Wherein he often meets
Old Wasters, Poets, Communists,
And Ladies from the Streets.)

A strong Protectionist, believes
In everything but Heaven.
For entertainment, dines, receives,
Unmarried, 57.

THE EXAMPLE

John Henderson, an unbeliever,
Had lately lost his Joie de Vivre
From reading far too many books.
He went about with gloomy looks;
Despair inhabited his breast
And made the man a perfect pest.
Not so his sister, Mary Lunn,
She had a whacking lot of fun!
Though unbelieving as a beast
She didn't worry in the least.
But drank as hard as she was able

And sang and danced upon the table;
And when she met her brother Jack
She used to smack him on the back
So smartly as to make him jump,
And cry, 'What-ho! You've got the hump!'
A phrase which, more than any other,
Was gall and wormwood to her brother;
For, having an agnostic mind,
He was exceedingly refined.
The Christians, a declining band,
Would point with monitory hand
To Henderson his desperation,
To Mary Lunn her dissipation,
And often mutter, 'Mark my words!
Something will happen to those birds!'
Which came to pass: for Mary Lunn
Died suddenly, at ninety-one,
Of Psittacosis, not before
Becoming an appalling bore.
While Henderson, I'm glad to state,
Though naturally celibate,
Married an intellectual wife
Who made him lead the Higher life
And wouldn't give him any wine;
Whereby he fell in a decline,
And, at the time of writing this,
Is suffering from paralysis,
The which, we hear with no surprise,
Will shortly end in his demise.

Moral
The moral is (it is indeed!)
You mustn't monkey with the Creed.

ON JAM

I write of Jam, a subject stiff
With interest to the reader if
He is (or she is), as am I,
From youth of Jam a votary.

Jam should be only eaten spread
By Nurse – or some one else – on bread.
A decent child would just as soon
Have none as eat it with a spoon.
And if you take it with your fingers,
There's always something sticks and lingers,
And visitors go muttering 'D . . . (Oh! look!)
The little brute's been eating Jam!'

Jam is of various sorts and kinds,
As – Apple (made of apple-rinds);
And Strawberry – of which the fruit
Recalls the luscious Turnip root;
And Cherry Jam – extremely rich;
And Currant and Banana (which
The Germans oddly love to eat
With Boiled and Baked and Roasted Meat);
And Quince (which is of Quinces, since
It otherwise could not be Quince);
And Marmalade – but that expression
Compels me to a short digression.

The haughty Nobles of Seville
Could make no use of Orange Peel
Until the Merchants of Dundee
Came sailing thither oversea,
And, steering up the noble river

Called, in their tongue, the Guadalquiver,
Took back the skins with them and made
The mixture known as Marmalade,
As popular as it can be
From Dingwall on the Northern Sea
To Cherrapunji in Assam –
But certainly is never Jam!

What is there more that I can say
Of Jam? Why, nothing more to-day.
The Jam's before me, thick and sweet:
What's writing, when a man can eat?
And as Erigena has said
(An author far too little read),
Jam hora adest ut mangiam.
And that is all I know of Jam.

LETTER ' FROM MY LITTLE HOUSE IN CHEYNE WALK' [TO E. V. LUCAS, 1904]

O, Lucas, *why* do you not come and see me?
You fence yourself with silence, hoping thus
As does the foolish ostrich of the desert
By shutting sense to turn the world away.
Of those blue buses which from Kensington
Run down the Earl's Court Road, th' alternate ones
Come to within two minutes of this house:
Those marked 'King's Road' – for those marked 'Redcliffe Arms'
Stop short, turn baffled, face the north, recoil
Long ere the goal be won. The fare is 2d.
You ask for *Milman's St*, a little street,
Quite short, and close to where the buses stop.
You go down this, and when you reach the river

Mine is the house upon the *left* hand side:
A little, aged, cracked, neglected house,
And painted white in front; but Home to me.
(Here follow lines upon the English Home.)
So, Lucas, come.

                Lucas, forswear ambition.
By that sin Angels fell, and how can you
That have not wings, nor night-gown nor blue eyes
Nor flaxen hair, nor anything at all
That appertains to angels, hope to win by it?
It is Ambition nails you to your house,
It is Ambition makes you take the bus
And visit London daily and neglect
The sacred duty of amusing me.
Lucas, when Brutus had Pneumonia
Caesar would call and sit beside his bed
And pat his hands and ask him how he did:
Did this in Caesar seem ambition?
Yet Caesar was an honourable man:
And you are more than Caesar, that did hold
Vast Fate and all the orb an Atlas bears,
His heritage of arms – that is until
On March the 15th, B.C. 44.
Close at the base of Pompey's statua,
Spouting thick Julian blood, while all the while
The senators were spouting rhetoric,
Great Caesar fell.

              (An interval for lunch)
  Now that I have eaten a pheasant, drunk a bottle
of Burgundy and put away a cigar I can write in
prose – but there is no doubt that in periods of weakness the unrhymed heroic pentameter is the easier
medium.

  Answer this.

THE LOSER

(An earlier version of the verses on p. 161)

He had a pair of silver studs
  That kept his cuffs from playing tricks;
He lost them . . . with some other duds . . .
  At Rome, in 1896.

He lost a lot of other things:
  His sword, his scabbard, and his spurs,
His medal, and a pair of rings . . .
  (And both of them, by God, were hers!)

He lost his innocence (of course!)
  The day before the flight began.
He lost his saddle and his horse,
  His bag, his bridle, and his man.

He lost his temper after that,
  And then he lost his lighter touch;
He lost his papers and his hat;
  He lost (it didn't hurt him much!)

His way of launching easy jests,
  His way of giving graceful praise,
His way of entertaining guests,
  His way of . . . all his little ways.

He lost his head completely, and
  He lost promotion for a cert.;
And, what was worse, he lost his hand
  By amputation, and it hurt.

He lost his money and his heart,
  His life, and didn't count the cost;
And even those who took his part
  Admitted that the man had lost –

His character, his care for truth,
  His honour and his self-control,
The love that graced his early youth,
  And lastly his immortal soul.

★

The grocer Hudson Kearley, he
When purchasing his barony
Considered, as we understand,
The title of Lord Sugarsand,
Or then again he could have been
Lord Underweight of Margarine,
But, being of the nobler sort,
He took the name of Devonport.

CAUTIONARY VERSES

Evelyn Bell.
I love you well.

THE BAD CHILD'S BOOK OF BEASTS

INTRODUCTION

I call you bad, my little child,
   Upon the title page,
Because a manner rude and wild
   Is common at your age.

The Moral of this priceless work
   (If rightly understood)
Will make you – from a little Turk –
   Unnaturally good.

Do not as evil children do,
   Who on the slightest grounds
Will imitate the Kangaroo,
   With wild unmeaning bounds:

Do not as children badly bred,
   Who eat like little Hogs,
And when they have to go to bed
   Will whine like Puppy Dogs:

Who take their manners from the Ape,
   Their habits from the Bear,
Indulge the loud unseemly jape,
   And never brush their hair.

But so control your actions that
   Your friends may all repeat,
'This child is dainty as the Cat,
   And as the Owl discreet.'

THE YAK

As a friend to the children commend me the Yak.
   You will find it exactly the thing:
It will carry and fetch, you can ride on its back,
   Or lead it about with a string.

The Tartar who dwells on the plains of Thibet
   (A desolate region of snow)
Has for centuries made it a nursery pet,
   And surely the Tartar should know!

Then tell your papa where the Yak can be got,
   And if he is awfully rich
He will buy you the creature – or else he will *not*.
   (I cannot be positive which.)

THE POLAR BEAR

The Polar Bear is unaware
   Of cold that cuts me through:
For why? He has a coat of hair.
   I wish I had one too!

THE LION

The Lion, the Lion, he dwells in the waste,
He has a big head and a very small waist;
But his shoulders are stark, and his jaws they are grim,
And a good little child will not play with him.

THE TIGER

The Tiger on the other hand, is kittenish and mild,
He makes a pretty playfellow for any little child;
And mothers of large families (who claim to common sense)
Will find a Tiger well repay the trouble and expense.

THE DROMEDARY

The Dromedary is a cheerful bird:
I cannot say the same about the Kurd.

THE WHALE

The Whale that wanders round the Pole
  Is not a table fish.
You cannot bake or boil him whole,
  Nor serve him in a dish;

But you may cut his blubber up
  And melt it down for oil,
And so replace the colza bean
  (A product of the soil).

These facts should all be noted down
  And ruminated on,
By every boy in Oxford town
  Who wants to be a Don.

THE HIPPOPOTAMUS

I shoot the Hippopotamus
With bullets made of platinum,
Because if I use leaden ones
His hide is sure to flatten 'em.

THE DODO

The Dodo used to walk around,
  And take the sun and air.
The sun yet warms his native ground –
  The Dodo is not there!

The voice which used to squawk and squeak
  Is now for ever dumb –
Yet may you see his bones and beak
  All in the Mu-se-um.

THE MARMOZET

The species Man and Marmozet
  Are intimately linked;
The Marmozet survives as yet,
  But Men are all extinct.

THE CAMELOPARD

The Camelopard, it is said
  By travellers (who never lie),
He cannot stretch out straight in bed
  Because he is so high.
The clouds surround his lofty head,
  His hornlets touch the sky.

How shall I hunt this quadruped?
  I cannot tell! Not I!
I'll buy a little parachute
  (A common parachute with wings),
I'll fill it full of arrowroot
  And other necessary things,

And I will slay this fearful brute
With stones and sticks and guns and slings.

THE LEARNED FISH

This learned Fish has not sufficient brains
To go into the water when it rains.

THE ELEPHANT

When people call this beast to mind
   They marvel more and more
At such a LITTLE tail behind,
   So LARGE a trunk before.

THE BIG BABOON

The Big Baboon is found upon
   The plains of Cariboo:
He goes about with nothing on
   (A shocking thing to do).

But if he dressed respectably
   And let his whiskers grow,
How like this Big Baboon would be
   To Mister So-and-so!

THE RHINOCEROS

Rhinoceros, your hide looks all undone,
You do not take my fancy in the least:
You have a horn where other brutes have none:
   Rhinoceros, you are an ugly beast.

THE FROG

Be kind and tender to the Frog,
   And do not call him names,
As 'Slimy skin,' or 'Polly-wog,'
   Or likewise 'Ugly James,'
Or 'Gape-a-grin,' or 'Toad-gone-wrong,'
   Or 'Billy Bandy-knees':

[239]

The Frog is justly sensitive
    To epithets like these.
No animal will more repay
    A treatment kind and fair;
At least so lonely people say
Who keep a frog (and, by the way,
They are extremely rare).

INTRODUCTION

The parents of the learned child
    (His father and his mother)
Were utterly aghast to note
The facts he would at random quote
On creatures curious, rare and wild;
    And wondering, asked each other:

'An idle little child like this,
    How is it that he knows
What years of close analysis
    Are powerless to disclose?

Our brains are trained, our books are big,
    And yet we always fail
To answer why the Guinea-pig
    Is born without a tail.

Or why the Wanderoo[1] should rant
    In wild, unmeaning rhymes,
Whereas the Indian Elephant
    Will only read *The Times*.

Perhaps he found a way to slip
    Unnoticed to the Zoo,
And gave the Pachyderm a tip,
    Or pumped the Wanderoo.

Or even by an artful plan
    Deceived our watchful eyes,
And interviewed the Pelican,
    Who is extremely wise.'

[1] Sometimes called the 'Lion-tailed or tufted Baboon of Ceylon.

'Oh! no,' said he, in humble tone,
  With shy but conscious look,
'Such facts I never could have known
  But for this little book.'

THE PYTHON

A Python I should not advise –
It needs a doctor for its eyes
And has the measles yearly.
However, if you feel inclined
To get one (to improve your mind,
And not from fashion merely),
Allow no music near its cage;
And when it flies into a rage
Chastise it, most severely.

I had an aunt in Yucatan
Who bought a Python from a man
  And kept it for a pet.
She died, because she never knew
Those simple little rules and few –
  The Snake is living yet.

THE WELSH MUTTON

The Cambrian Welsh or Mountain Sheep
  Is of the Ovine race,
His conversation is not deep,
  But then – observe his face!

THE PORCUPINE

What! would you slap the Porcupine?
　Unhappy child – desist!
Alas! that any friend of mine
　Should turn Tupto-philist.[1]

To strike the meanest and the least
　Of creatures is a sin,
How much more bad to beat a beast
　With prickles on its skin.

THE SCORPION

The Scorpion is as black as soot,
　He dearly loves to bite;
He is a most unpleasant brute
　To find in bed, at night.

THE CROCODILE

Whatever our faults, we can always engage
That no fancy or fable shall sully our page,
　So take note of what follows, I beg.
This creature so grand and august in its age,
　In its youth is hatched out of an egg.
And oft in some far Coptic town
The Missionary sits him down
　To breakfast by the Nile:
The heart beneath his priestly gown
　Is innocent of guile;
When suddenly the rigid frown
Of Panic is observed to drown
　His customary smile.

[1] From τύπτω = I strike; φιλέω = I love; one that loves to strike. The word is not found in classical Greek, nor does it occur among the writers of the Renaissance – nor anywhere else.

Why does he start and leap amain,
And scour the sandy Libyan plain
Like one that wants to catch a train,
Or wrestles with internal pain?
Because he finds his egg contain –
Green, hungry, horrible and plain –
    An Infant Crocodile.

THE VULTURE

The Vulture eats between his meals,
    And that's the reason why
He very, very rarely feels
    As well as you and I.

His eye is dull, his head is bald,
    His neck is growing thinner.
Oh! what a lesson for us all
    To only eat at dinner!

THE BISON

The Bison is vain, and (I write it with pain)
    The Door-mat you see on his head
Is not, as some learned professors maintain,
The opulent growth of a genius' brain;
    But is sewn on with needle and thread.

THE VIPER

Yet another great truth I record in my verse,
That some Vipers are venomous, some the reverse;
    A fact you may prove if you try,
By procuring two Vipers, and letting them bite;
With the *first* you are only the worse for a fright,
    But after the *second* you die.

THE LLAMA

The Llama is a woolly sort of fleecy hairy goat,
With an indolent expression and an undulating throat
   Like an unsuccessful literary man.
And I know the place he lives in (or at least – I think I do)
It is Ecuador, Brazil or Chile – possibly Peru;
   You must find it in the Atlas if you can.
The Llama of the Pampasses you never should confound
(In spite of a deceptive similarity of sound)
   With the Lama who is Lord of Turkestan.
For the former is a beautiful and valuable beast,
But the latter is not lovable nor useful in the least;
And the Ruminant is preferable surely to the Priest
Who battens on the woful superstitions of the East,
   The Mongol of the Monastery of Shan.

THE CHAMOIS

The Chamois inhabits
Lucerne, where his habits
   (Though why I have not an idea-r)
Give him sudden short spasms
On the brink of deep chasms,
   And he lives in perpetual fear.

THE FROZEN MAMMOTH

This Creature, though rare, is still found to the East
Of the Northern Siberian Zone.
It is known to the whole of that primitive group
That the carcass will furnish an excellent soup,
   Though the cooking it offers one drawback at least
     (Of a serious nature I own):

[245]

If the skin be *but punctured* before it is boiled,
Your confection is wholly and utterly spoiled.
And hence (on account of the size of the beast)
    The dainty is nearly unknown.

THE MICROBE

The Microbe is so very small
You cannot make him out at all,
But many sanguine people hope
To see him through a microscope.
His jointed tongue that lies beneath
A hundred curious rows of teeth;
His seven tufted tails with lots
Of lovely pink and purple spots,
On each of which a pattern stands,
Composed of forty separate bands;
His eyebrows of a tender green;
All these have never yet been seen –
But Scientists, who ought to know,
Assure us that they must be so . . .
Oh! let us never, never doubt
What nobody is sure about!

A MORAL ALPHABET

A stands for Archibald who told no lies,
And got this lovely volume for a prize.
The Upper School had combed and oiled their hair,
And all the Parents of the Boys were there.
In words that ring like thunder through the Hall,
Draw tears from some and loud applause from all, –
The Pedagogue, with Pardonable Joy,
Bestows the Gift upon the Radiant Boy: –
'Accept the Noblest Work produced as yet'
(Says he) 'upon the English Alphabet;
Next term I shall examine you, to find
If you have read it thoroughly. So mind!'
And while the Boys and Parents cheered so loud,
That out of doors a large and anxious crowd
Had gathered and was blocking up the street,
The admirable child resumed his seat.

MORAL
Learn from this justly irritating Youth,
To brush your Hair and Teeth and tell the Truth.

B stands for Bear. When Bears are seen
    Approaching in the distance,
Make up your mind at once between
    Retreat and Armed Resistance.

A Gentleman remained to fight –
    With what result for him?
The Bear, with ill-concealed delight,
    Devoured him, Limb by Limb.

Another Person turned and ran;
    He ran extremely hard:
The Bear was faster than the Man,
    And beat him by a yard.

MORAL

Decisive action in the hour of need
Denotes the Hero, but does not succeed.

C stands for Cobra; when the Cobra bites
An Indian Judge, the Judge spends restless nights.

MORAL

This creature, though disgusting and appalling,
Conveys no kind of Moral worth recalling.

D The Dreadful Dinotherium he
Will have to do his best for D.
The early world observed with awe
His back, indented like a saw.
His look was gay, his voice was strong;
His tail was neither short nor long;
His trunk, or elongated nose,
Was not so large as some suppose;
His teeth, as all the world allows,
Were graminivorous, like a cow's.
He therefore should have wished to pass
Long peaceful nights upon the Grass,
But being mad the brute preferred

To roost in branches, like a bird.[1]
A creature heavier than a whale,
You see at once, could hardly fail
To suffer badly when he slid
And tumbled (as he always did).
His fossil, therefore, comes to light
All broken up: and serve him right.

MORAL

If you were born to walk the ground,
Remain there; do not fool around.

E stands for Egg.

MORAL

The Moral of this verse
Is applicable to the Young. Be terse.

F for a Family taking a walk
 In Arcadia Terrace, no doubt:
The parents indulge in intelligent talk,
 While the children they gambol about.

At a quarter-past six they return to their tea,
Of a kind that would hardly be tempting to me,
 Though my appetite passes belief.

---

[1] We have good reason to suppose
He did so, from his claw-like toes.

There is Jam, Ginger Beer, Buttered Toast, Marmalade,
With a Cold Leg of Mutton and Warm Lemonade,
And a large Pigeon Pie very skilfully made
    To consist almost wholly of Beef.

MORAL

A Respectable Family taking the air
   Is a subject on which I could dwell;
It contains all the morals that ever there were,
   And it sets an example as well.

G stands for Gnu, whose weapons of Defence
Are long, sharp, curling Horns, and Common-sense.
To these he adds a Name so short and strong
That even Hardy Boers pronounce it wrong.
How often on a bright Autumnal day
The Pious people of Pretoria say,
'Come, let us hunt the –' Then no more is heard
But Sounds of Strong Men struggling with a word.
Meanwhile, the distant Gnu with grateful eyes
Observes his opportunity, and flies.

MORAL

   Child, if you have a rummy kind of name,
   Remember to be thankful for the same.

H was a Horseman who rode to the meet,
And talked of the Pads of the fox as his 'feet' –
An error which furnished subscribers with grounds
For refusing to make him a Master of Hounds.

[250]

He gave way thereupon to so fearful a rage,
That he sold up his Stable and went on the Stage,
And had all the success that a man could desire
In creating the part of 'The Old English Squire.'

MORAL
In the Learned Professions, a person should know
The advantage of having two strings to his bow.

I the Poor Indian, justly called 'The Poor,'
He has to eat his Dinner off the floor.

MORAL
The Moral these delightful lines afford
Is: 'Living cheaply is its own reward.'

J stands for James, who thought it immaterial
To pay his taxes, Local or Imperial.
In vain the Mother wept, the Wife implored,
James only yawned as though a trifle bored.
The Tax Collector called again, but he
Was met with Persiflage and Repartee.
When James was hauled before the learned Judge,
Who lectured him, he loudly whispered, 'Fudge!'
The Judge was startled from his usual calm,
He struck the desk before him with his palm,
And roared in tones to make the boldest quail,
'*J stands for James,* IT ALSO STANDS FOR JAIL.'
And therefore, on a dark and dreadful day,
Policemen came and took him all away.

The fate of James is typical, and shows
How little mercy people can expect
Who will not pay their taxes; (saving those
To which they conscientiously object.)

K for the Klondyke, a Country of Gold,
Where the winters are often excessively cold;
Where the lawn every morning is covered with rime,
And skating continues for years at a time.
Do you think that a Climate can conquer the grit
Of the Sons of the West? Not a bit! Not a bit!
When the weather looks nippy, the bold Pioneers
Put on two pairs of Stockings and cover their ears,
And roam through the drear Hyperborean dales
With a vast apparatus of Buckets and Pails;
Or wander through wild Hyperborean glades
With Hoes, Hammers, Pickaxes, Mattocks and Spades.
There are some who give rise to exuberant mirth
By turning up nothing but bushels of earth,
While those who have little cause excellent fun
By attempting to pilfer from those who have none.
At times the reward they will get for their pains
Is to strike very tempting auriferous veins;
Or, a shaft being sunk for some miles in the ground,
Not infrequently nuggets of value are found.
They bring us the gold when their labours are ended,
And we – after thanking them prettily – spend it.

MORAL

Just you work for Humanity, never you mind
If Humanity seems to have left you behind.

L was a Lady, Advancing in Age,
 Who drove in her carriage and six,
With a Couple of Footmen, a Coachman and Page,
 Who were all of them regular bricks.
If the Coach ran away, or was smashed by a Dray,
 Or got into collisions and blocks,
The Page, with a courtesy rare for his years,
Would leap to the ground with inspiriting cheers,
While the Footman allayed her legitimate fears,
 And the Coachman sat tight on his box.
At night as they met round an excellent meal,
 They would take it in turn to observe:
'What a Lady indeed! . . . what a presence to feel! . . .'
 'What a Woman to worship and serve! . . .'
But, perhaps, the most poignant of all their delights
 Was to stand in a rapturous Dream
When she spoke to them kindly on Saturday Nights,
 And said 'They deserved her Esteem.'

MORAL

Now observe the Reward of these dutiful lives:
 At the end of their Loyal Career
They each had a Lodge at the end of the drives,
 And she left them a Hundred a Year.
Remember from this to be properly vexed
 When the newspaper editors say
That 'The type of society shown in the Text
 Is rapidly passing away.'

M was a Millionaire who sat at Table,
    And ate like this – as long as he was able;
At half-past twelve the waiters turned him out:
    He lived impoverished and died of gout.

MORAL

Disgusting exhibition! Have a care
When, later on, you are a Millionaire,
To rise from table feeling you could still
Take something more, and not be really ill.

N stands for Ned, Maria's younger brother,
Who, walking one way, chose to gaze the other.
In Blandford Square – a crowded part of town –
Two People on a tandem knocked him down;
Whereat a Motor Car, with warning shout,
Ran right on top and turned him inside out:
The damages that he obtained from these
Maintained him all his life in cultured ease.

MORAL

The law protects you. Go your gentle way:
The Other Man has always got to Pay.

O stands for Oxford. Hail! salubrious seat
Of learning! Academical Retreat!
Home of my Middle Age! Malarial Spot
Which People call Medeeval (though it's not).

The marshes in the neighbourhood can vie
With Cambridge, but the town itself is dry,
And serves to make a kind of Fold or Pen
Wherein to herd a lot of Learned Men.
Were I to write but half of what they know,
It would exhaust the space reserved for 'O';
And, as my book must not be over big,
I turn at once to 'P', which stands for Pig.

MORAL

Be taught by this to speak with moderation
Of places where, with decent application,
One gets a good, sound, middle-class education.

P stands for Pig, as I remarked before,
A second cousin to the Huge Wild Boar.
But Pigs are civilised, while Huge Wild Boars
Live savagely, at random, out of doors,
And, in their coarse contempt for dainty foods,
Subsist on Truffles, which they find in woods.
Not so the cultivated Pig, who feels
The need of several courses at his meals,
But wrongly thinks it does not matter whether
He takes them one by one or all together.
Hence, Pigs devour, from lack of self-respect,
What Epicures would certainly eject.

MORAL

Learn from the Pig to take whatever Fate
Or Elder Persons heap upon your plate.

Q for Quinine, which children take
With Jam and little bits of cake.

MORAL
How idiotic! Can Quinine
Replace Cold Baths and Sound Hygiene?

R the Reviewer, reviewing my book,
At which he had barely intended to look;
But the very first lines upon 'A' were enough
To convince him the Verses were excellent stuff.
So he wrote, without stopping, for several days
In terms of extreme but well-merited Praise.
To quote but one Passage: 'No Person' (says he)
'Will be really content without purchasing three,
While a Parent will send for a dozen or more,
And strew them about on the Nursery Floor.
The Versification might call for some strictures
Were it not for its singular wit; while the Pictures,
Tho' the handling of line is a little defective,
Make up amply in *verve* what they lack in perspective.'

MORAL
The habit of constantly telling the Truth
Will lend an additional lustre to Youth.

S stands for Snail, who, though he be the least,
Is not an uninstructive Hornèd Beast.
His eyes are on his Horns, and when you shout
Or tickle them, the Horns go in and out.

[256]

Had Providence seen proper to endow
The furious Unicorn or sober Cow
With such a gift, the one would never now
Appear so commonplace on Coats of Arms.
And what a fortune for our failing farms
If circus managers, with wealth untold,
Would take the Cows for half their weight in gold!

MORAL
Learn from the Snail to take reproof with patience,
And not put out your Horns on all occasions.

T for the Genial Tourist, who resides
In Peckham, where he writes Italian Guides.

MORAL
Learn from this information not to cavil
At slight mistakes in books on foreign travel.

U for the Upas Tree, that casts a blight
On those that pull their sisters' hair, and fight.
But oh! the Good! They wander undismayed,
And (as the Subtle Artist has portrayed)
Dispend the golden hours at play beneath its shade.[1]

MORAL
Dear Reader, if you chance to catch a sight
Of Upas Trees, betake yourself to flight.

[1] A friend of mine, a Botanist, believes
   The Good can even browse upon its leaves.
   I doubt it . . .

[257]

V for the unobtrusive Volunteer,
Who fills the Armies of the World with fear.

MORAL
Seek with the Volunteer to put aside
The empty Pomp of Military Pride.

My little victim, let me trouble you
To fix your active mind on W.
The Waterbeetle here shall teach
A sermon far beyond your reach:
He flabbergasts the Human Race
By gliding on the water's face
With ease, celerity, and grace;
But if he ever stopped to think
Of how he did it, he would sink.

MORAL
Don't ask Questions!

No reasonable little Child expects
A Grown-up Man to make a rhyme on X.

MORAL
These verses teach a clever child to find
Excuse for doing all that he's inclined.

[258]

Y stands for Youth (it would have stood for Yak,
But that I wrote about him two years back).
Youth is the pleasant springtime of our days,
As Dante so mellifluously says
(Who always speaks of Youth with proper praise).
You have not got to Youth, but when you do
You'll find what He and I have said is true.

MORAL

Youth's excellence should teach the Modern Wit
First to be Young, and then to boast of it.

Z for this Zébu, who (like all Zebús)[1]
Is held divine by scrupulous Hindoos.

MORAL

Idolatry, as you are well aware,
Is highly reprehensible. But there,
We needn't bother, – when we get to Z
Our interest in the Alphabet is dead.

[1] Von Kettner writes it 'Zébu'; Wurst 'Zebú';
  I split the difference and use the two.

CAUTIONARY TALES FOR CHILDREN

JIM
WHO RAN AWAY FROM HIS NURSE, AND WAS EATEN BY A LION

There was a Boy whose name was Jim;
His Friends were very good to him.
They gave him Tea, and Cakes, and Jam,
And slices of delicious Ham,
And Chocolate with pink inside,
And little Tricycles to ride,
And read him Stories through and through,
And even took him to the Zoo –
But there it was the dreadful Fate
Befell him, which I now relate.

You know – at least you ought to know,
For I have often told you so –
That Children never are allowed
To leave their Nurses in a Crowd;
Now this was Jim's especial Foible,
He ran away when he was able,
And on this inauspicious day
He slipped his hand and ran away!
He hadn't gone a yard when – Bang!
With open Jaws, a Lion sprang,
And hungrily began to eat
The Boy: beginning at his feet.

Now, just imagine how it feels
When first your toes and then your heels,
And then by gradual degrees,
Your shins and ankles, calves and knees,

Are slowly eaten, bit by bit.
No wonder Jim detested it!
No wonder that he shouted 'Hi'!
The Honest Keeper heard his cry,
Though very fat he almost ran
To help the little gentleman.
'Ponto!' he ordered as he came
(For Ponto was the Lion's name),
'Ponto!' he cried, with angry Frown.
'Let go, Sir! Down, Sir! Put it down!'

The Lion made a sudden Stop,
He let the Dainty Morsel drop,
And slunk reluctant to his Cage,
Snarling with Disappointed Rage.
But when he bent him over Jim,
The Honest Keeper's Eyes were dim.
The Lion having reached his Head,
The Miserable Boy was dead!
When Nurse informed his Parents, they
Were more Concerned than I can say: –
His Mother, as she dried her eyes,
Said, 'Well – it gives me no surprise,
He would not do as he was told!'
His Father, who was self-controlled,
Bade all the children round attend
To James' miserable end,
And always keep a-hold of Nurse
For fear of finding something worse.

WHO CHEWED BITS OF STRING, AND WAS
EARLY CUT OFF IN DREADFUL AGONIES

The Chief Defect of Henry King
    Was chewing little bits of String.
At last he swallowed some which tied
    Itself in ugly Knots inside.
Physicians of the Utmost Fame
Were called at once; but when they came
They answered, as they took their Fees,
'There is no Cure for this Disease.
Henry will very soon be dead.'
His Parents stood about his Bed
Lamenting his Untimely Death,
When Henry, with his Latest Breath,
Cried – 'Oh, my Friends, be warned by me,
That Breakfast, Dinner, Lunch, and Tea
Are all the Human Frame requires . . .'
With that, the Wretched Child expires.

MATILDA
WHO TOLD LIES, AND WAS BURNED TO DEATH

Matilda told such Dreadful Lies,
It made one Gasp and Stretch one's Eyes;
Her Aunt, who, from her Earliest Youth,
Had kept a Strict Regard for Truth,
Attempted to Believe Matilda:
The effort very nearly killed her,
And would have done so, had not She
Discovered this Infirmity.
For once, towards the Close of Day,
Matilda, growing tired of play,

And finding she was left alone,
Went tiptoe to the Telephone
And summoned the Immediate Aid
Of London's Noble Fire-Brigade.
Within an hour the Gallant Band
Were pouring in on every hand,
From Putney, Hackney Downs, and Bow
With Courage high and Hearts a-glow
They galloped, roaring through the Town,
'Matilda's House is Burning Down!'
Inspired by British Cheers and Loud
Proceeding from the Frenzied Crowd,
They ran their ladders through a score
Of windows on the Ball Room Floor;
And took Peculiar Pains to Souse
The Pictures up and down the House,
Until Matilda's Aunt succeeded
In showing them they were not needed;
And even then she had to pay
To get the Men to go away!

     .   .   .

It happened that a few Weeks later
Her Aunt was off to the Theatre
To see that Interesting Play
The Second Mrs Tanqueray.
She had refused to take her Niece
To hear this Entertaining Piece:
A Deprivation Just and Wise
To Punish her for Telling Lies.
That Night a Fire *did* break out –
You should have heard Matilda Shout!
You should have heard her Scream and Bawl,
And throw the window up and call
To People passing in the Street –

(The rapidly increasing Heat
Encouraging her to obtain
Their confidence) – but all in vain!
For every time She shouted 'Fire!'
They only answered 'Little Liar'!
And therefore when her Aunt returned,
Matilda, and the House, were Burned.

FRANKLIN HYDE
WHO CAROUSED IN THE DIRT AND WAS CORRECTED BY HIS UNCLE

His Uncle came on Franklin Hyde
Carousing in the Dirt.
He Shook him hard from Side to Side
And Hit him till it Hurt,
Exclaiming, with a Final Thud,
'Take that! Abandoned Boy!
For Playing with Disgusting Mud
As though it were a Toy!'

MORAL

From Franklin Hyde's adventure, learn
To pass your Leisure Time
In Cleanly Merriment, and turn
From Mud and Ooze and Slime
And every form of Nastiness –
But, on the other Hand,
Children in ordinary Dress
May always play with Sand.

GODOLPHIN HORNE
WHO WAS CURSED WITH THE SIN OF PRIDE,
AND BECAME A BOOT-BLACK

Godolphin Horne was Nobly Born;
He held the Human Race in Scorn,
And lived with all his Sisters where
His Father lived, in Berkeley Square.
And oh! the Lad was Deathly Proud!
He never shook your Hand or Bowed,
But merely smirked and nodded thus:
How perfectly ridiculous!
Alas! That such Affected Tricks
Should flourish in a Child of Six!
(For such was Young Godolphin's age).
Just then, the Court required a Page,
Whereat the Lord High Chamberlain
(The Kindest and the Best of Men),
He went good-naturedly and took
A Perfectly Enormous Book
Called *People Qualified to Be*
Attendant on His Majesty,
And murmured, as he scanned the list
(To see that no one should be missed),
'There's William Coutts has got the Flu,
And Billy Higgs would never do,
And Guy de Vere is far too young,
And . . . wasn't D'Alton's Father hung?
And as for Alexander Byng! – . . .
I think I know the kind of thing,
A Churchman, cleanly, nobly born,
Come let us say Godolphin Horne?'
But hardly had he said the word
When Murmurs of Dissent were heard.
The King of Iceland's Eldest Son

Said, 'Thank you! I am taking none!'
The Aged Duchess of Athlone
Remarked, in her sub-acid tone,
'I doubt if He is what we need!'
With which the Bishops all agreed;
And even Lady Mary Flood
(So Kind, and oh! so *really* good)
Said, 'No! He wouldn't do at all,
He'd make us feel a lot too small.'
The Chamberlain said, ' . . . Well, well, well!
No doubt you're right . . . One cannot tell!'
He took his Gold and Diamond Pen
And Scratched Godolphin out again.
So now Godolphin is the Boy
Who blacks the Boots at the Savoy.

ALGERNON

WHO PLAYED WITH A LOADED GUN, AND,
ON MISSING HIS SISTER, WAS REPRIMANDED
BY HIS FATHER

Young Algernon, the Doctor's Son,
Was playing with a Loaded Gun.
He pointed it towards his sister,
Aimed very carefully, but Missed her!
His Father, who was standing near,
The Loud Explosion chanced to Hear,
And reprimanded Algernon
For playing with a Loaded Gun.

'Oh Murder! What was that, Papa!'
'My child, it was a Motor-Car,
A Most Ingenious Toy!
Designed to Captivate and Charm
Much rather than to rouse Alarm
In any English Boy.

'What would your Great Grandfather who
Was Aide-de-Camp to General Brue,
And lost a leg at Waterloo,
And Quatre-Bras and Ligny too!
And died at Trafalgar! –
What would he have remarked to hear
His Young Descendant shriek with fear,
Because he happened to be near
    A Harmless Motor-Car!
But do not fret about it! Come!
We'll off to Town and purchase some!'

REBECCA
WHO SLAMMED DOORS FOR FUN AND
PERISHED MISERABLY

A Trick that everyone abhors
In Little Girls is slamming Doors,
A Wealthy Banker's Little Daughter
Who lived in Palace Green, Bayswater
(By name Rebecca Offendort),
Was given to this Furious Sport.

She would deliberately go
And Slam the door like Billy-Ho!
To make her Uncle Jacob start.
She was not really bad at heart,
But only rather rude and wild:
She was an aggravating child . . .

It happened that a Marble Bust
Of Abraham was standing just
Above the Door this little Lamb
Had carefully prepared to Slam,
And Down it came! It knocked her flat!
It laid her out! She looked like that.

   .   .   .

Her funeral Sermon (which was long
And followed by a Sacred Song)
Mentioned her Virtues, it is true,
But dwelt upon her Vices too,
And showed the Dreadful End of One
Who goes and slams the door for Fun.

   .   .   .

The children who were brought to hear
The awful Tale from far and near
Were much impressed, and inly swore
They never more would slam the Door.
– As often they had done before.

GEORGE
WHO PLAYED WITH A DANGEROUS TOY, AND SUFFERED A CATASTROPHE OF CONSIDERABLE DIMENSIONS

When George's Grandmamma was told
That George had been as good as Gold,
She Promised in the Afternoon
To buy him an Immense BALLOON.
And so she did; but when it came,
It got into the candle flame,
And being of a dangerous sort
Exploded with a loud report!

The Lights went out! The Windows broke!
The Room was filled with reeking smoke.
And in the darkness shrieks and yells
Were mingled with Electric Bells,
And falling masonry and groans,
And crunching, as of broken bones,
And dreadful shrieks, when, worst of all,
The House itself began to fall!
It tottered, shuddering to and fro,
Then crashed into the street below –
Which happened to be Savile Row.

.   .   .

When Help arrived, among the Dead
Were Cousin Mary, Little Fred,
The Footmen (both of them), The Groom,
The man that cleaned the Billiard-Room,
The Chaplain, and the Still-Room Maid.
And I am dreadfully afraid
That Monsieur Champignon, the Chef,
Will now be permanently deaf –

And both his Aides are much the same;
While George, who was in part to blame,
Received, you will regret to hear,
A nasty lump behind the ear.

The moral is that little Boys
Should not be given dangerous Toys.

CHARLES AUGUSTUS FORTESCUE
WHO ALWAYS DID WHAT WAS RIGHT, AND SO ACCUMULATED AN IMMENSE FORTUNE

The nicest child I ever knew
Was Charles Augustus Fortescue.
He never lost his cap, or tore
His stockings or his pinafore:
    In eating Bread he made no Crumbs,
    He was extremely fond of sums,
To which, however, he preferred
The Parsing of a Latin Word –
He sought, when it was in his power,
For information twice an hour,
And as for finding Mutton-Fat
Unappetising, far from that!
He often, at his Father's Board,
Would beg them, of his own accord,
To give him, if they did not mind,
The Greasiest Morsels they could find –
His Later Years did not belie
The Promise of his Infancy.
In Public Life he always tried
To take a judgment Broad and Wide;

In Private, none was more than he
Renowned for quiet courtesy.
He rose at once in his Career,
And long before his Fortieth Year
Had wedded Fifi, Only Child
Of Bunyan, First Lord Aberfylde.
He thus became immensely Rich,
And built the Splendid Mansion which
Is called 'The Cedars, Muswell Hill,'
Where he resides in Affluence still
To show what Everybody might
Become by SIMPLY DOING RIGHT.

A REPROOF OF GLUTTONY

The Elephant will eat of hay
Some four and twenty tons a day,
And in his little eyes express
His unaffected thankfulness
That Providence should deign to find
Him food of this delicious kind.
While they that pay for all the hay
Will frequently be heard to say
How highly privileged they feel
To help him make so large a meal.
The Boa Constrictor dotes on goats;
The Horse is quite content with oats,
Or will alternatively pass
A happy morning munching grass.
The great Ant Eater of Taluz
Consumes – or people say he does –
Not only what his name implies
But even ordinary flies:
And Marmosets and Chimpanzees
Are happy on the nuts of trees.
The Lion from the burning slopes
Of Atlas lives on Antelopes,
And only adds the flesh of men
By way of relish now and then;
As Cheetahs – yes, and Tigers, too,
And Jaguars of the Andes – do.
The Lobster, I have heard it said,
Eats nobody till he is dead;
And Cobras, though they have the sense
To poison you in self-defence,
Restrict their food to birds and hares:

Which also may be true of Bears.
Indeed wherever we survey
Our Humble Friends we find that they
Confine their appetites to what
May happen to be on the spot.
Simplicity and moderation
Distinguish all the Brute Creation.
But Man – proud man – (as Dryden sings)
Though wolfing quantities of things –
Smoked Salmon in transparent slices,
And Turbot à la Reine, and Ices,
And Truffled Pies and Caviare,
And Chinese Ginger from the Jar;
And Oysters; and a kind of stuff
Called Cassouletto (good enough!)
And Mutton duly steeped in claret
(Or jumped with young shallot and carrot),
And Chicken Livers done with rice,
And Quails (which, I am told, are Mice),
And Peaches from a sunny wall,
And – Lord! I don't know what and all! –
Oh! Yes! And Sausages – is not
Contented with his Prandial lot.

MORAL

The Moral is (I think, at least)
That Man is an UNGRATEFUL BEAST.

MARIA
WHO MADE FACES AND A DEPLORABLE
MARRIAGE

Maria loved to pull a face:
And no such commonplace grimace
As you or I or anyone

[273]

Might make at grandmamma for fun.
But one where nose and mouth and all
Were screwed into a kind of ball,
The which – as you may well expect –
Produced a horrible effect
On those it was directed at.
One morning she was struck like that! –
Her features took their final mould
In shapes that made your blood run cold
And wholly lost their former charm.
Mamma, in agonised alarm,
Consulted a renowned Masseuse
– An old and valued friend of hers –
Who rubbed the wretched child for days
In five and twenty different ways
And after that began again.
But all in vain! – But all in vain!
The years advance: Maria grows
Into a Blooming English Rose –
With every talent, every grace
(Save in this trifle of the face).
She sang, recited, laughed and played
At all that an accomplished maid
Should play with skill to be of note –
Golf, the Piano, and the Goat;
She talked in French till all was blue
And knew a little German too.
She told the tales that soldiers tell,
She also danced extremely well,
Her wit was pointed, loud and raw,
She shone at laying down the law,
She drank liqueurs instead of tea,
Her verse was admirably free
And quoted in the latest books –
But people couldn't stand her looks.

Her parents had with thoughtful care
Proclaimed her genius everywhere,
Nor quite concealed a wealth which sounds
Enormous – thirty million pounds –
And further whispered it that she
Could deal with it exclusively.
They did not hide her chief defect,
But what with birth and intellect
And breeding and such ample means,
And still in her delightful 'teens,
A girl like our Maria (they thought)
Should make the kind of match she ought.
Those who had seen her here at home
Might hesitate: but Paris? Rome? . . .
– The foreigners should take the bait.
And so they did. At any rate,
The greatest men of every land
Arrived in shoals to seek her hand,
Grand Dukes, Commanders of the Fleece,
Mysterious Millionaires from Greece,
And exiled Kings in large amounts,
Ambassadors and Papal Counts,
And Rastaquouères from Palamerez
And Famous Foreign Secretaries,
They came along in turns to call
But *all* – without exception, *all* –
Though with determination set,
Yet, when they actually *met*,
Would start convulsively as though
They had received a sudden blow,
And mumbling a discreet good-day
Would shuffle, turn and slink away.

The upshot of it was Maria
Was married to a neighbouring Squire

Who, being blind, could never guess
His wife's appalling ugliness.
The man was independent, dull,
Offensive, poor and masterful.
It was a very dreadful thing! . . .
Now let us turn to Sarah Byng.

SARAH BYNG
WHO COULD NOT READ AND WAS TOSSED
INTO A THORNY HEDGE BY A BULL

Some years ago you heard me sing
My doubts on Alexander Byng.
His sister Sarah now inspires
My jaded Muse, my failing fires.
Of Sarah Byng the tale is told
How when the child was twelve years old
She could not read or write a line.
Her sister Jane, though barely nine,
Could spout the Catechism through
And parts of Matthew Arnold too,
While little Bill who came between
Was quite unnaturally keen
On 'Athalie', by Jean Racine.
But not so Sarah! Not so Sal!
She was a most uncultured girl
Who didn't care a pinch of snuff
For any literary stuff
And gave the classics all a miss.
Observe the consequence of this!
As she was walking home one day,
Upon the fields across her way
A gate, securely padlocked, stood,
And by its side a piece of wood

On which was painted plain and full,
BEWARE THE VERY FURIOUS BULL
Alas! The young illiterate
Went blindly forward to her fate,
And ignorantly climbed the gate!
Now happily the Bull that day
Was rather in the mood for play
Than goring people through and through
As Bulls so very often do;
He tossed her lightly with his horns
Into a prickly hedge of thorns,
And stood by laughing while she strode
And pushed and struggled to the road.
The lesson was not lost upon
The child, who since has always gone
A long way round to keep away
From signs, whatever they may say,
And leaves a padlocked gate alone.
Moreover she has wisely grown
Confirmed in her instinctive guess
That literature breeds distress.

JACK AND HIS PONY, TOM

Jack had a little pony – Tom;
He frequently would take it from
The stable where it used to stand
And give it sugar with his hand.
He also gave it oats and hay
And carrots twenty times a day
And grass in basketfuls, and greens,
And swedes and mangolds also beans
And patent foods from various sources
And bread (which isn't good for horses)
And chocolate and apple-rings

And lots and lots of other things
The most of which do not agree
With Polo Ponies such as he.
And all in such a quantity
As ruined his digestion wholly
And turned him from a Ponopoly
– I mean a Polo Pony – into
A case that clearly must be seen to.
Because he swelled and swelled and swelled.
Which, when the kindly boy beheld,
He gave him medicine by the pail
And malted milk, and nutmeg ale,
And yet it only swelled the more
Until its stomach touched the floor,
And then it heaved and groaned as well
And staggered, till at last it fell
And found it could not rise again.
Jack wept and prayed – but all in vain.
The pony died, and as it died,
Kicked him severely in the side.

MORAL
Kindness to animals should be
Attuned to their brutality.

TOM AND HIS PONY, JACK

Tom had a little pony, Jack:
He vaulted lightly on its back
And galloped off for miles and miles,
A-leaping hedges, gates and stiles,
And shouting 'Yoicks!' and 'Tally-Ho!'
And 'Heads I win!' and 'Tails below!'
And many another sporting phrase.
He rode like this for several days,

Until the pony, feeling tired,
Collapsed, looked heavenward and expired.
His father made a fearful row.
He said 'By Gum, you've done it now!
Here lies – a carcase on the ground –
No less than five and twenty pound!
Indeed the value of the beast
Would probably have much increased.
His teeth were false; and all were told
That he was only four years old.
Oh! Curse it all! I tell you plain
I'll never let you ride again.'

MORAL
His father died when he was twenty
And left three horses, which is plenty.

ABOUT JOHN WHO LOST A FORTUNE BY
THROWING STONES

John Vavassour de Quentin Jones
Was very fond of throwing stones
At Horses, People, Passing Trains,
But 'specially at Window-panes.
Like many of the Upper Class
He liked the Sound of Broken Glass[1]
It bucked him up and made him gay:
It was his favourite form of Play.
But the Amusement cost him dear,
My children, as you now shall hear.

John Vavassour de Quentin had
An uncle, who adored the lad:
And often chuckled; 'Wait until

[1] A line I stole with subtle daring
From Wing-Commander Maurice Baring.

You see what's left you in my will!'
Nor were the words without import,
Because this uncle did a sort
Of something in the City, which
Had made him fabulously rich.
(Although his brother, John's papa,
Was poor, as many fathers are.)
He had a lot of stocks and shares
And half a street in Buenos Aires[1]
A bank in Rio, and a line
Of Steamers to the Argentine.
And options more than I can tell,
And bits of Canada as well;
He even had a mortgage on
The House inhabited by John.
His will, the cause of all the fuss,
Was carefully indited thus:

   'This is the last and solemn Will
Of Uncle William – known as Bill.
I do bequeath, devise and give
By Execution Mandative
The whole amount of what I've got
(It comes to a tremendous lot!)
In seizin to devolve upon
My well-beloved nephew John.
(And here the witnesses will sign
Their names upon the dotted line.)'
   Such was the Legal Instrument
Expressing Uncle Bill's intent.

   As time went on declining Health
Transmogrified this Man of Wealth;

[1] But this pronunciation varies
Some people call it Bu-enos Airés.

And it was excellently clear
That Uncle Bill's demise was near.

At last his sole idea of fun
Was sitting snoozling in the sun.
So once, when he would take the air,
They wheeled him in his Patent Chair
(By 'They,' I mean his Nurse, who came
From Dorchester upon the Thame:
Miss Charming was the Nurse's name).
To where beside a little wood
A long abandoned green-house stood,
And there he sank into a doze
Of senile and inept repose.
But not for long his drowsy ease!
A stone came whizzing through the trees,
And caught him smartly in the eye.
He woke with an appalling cry,
And shrieked in agonizing tones:
'Oh! Lord! Whoever's throwing stones!'
Miss Charming, who was standing near,
Said: 'That was Master John, I fear!'
'Go, get my Ink-pot and my Quill,
My Blotter and my Famous Will.'
Miss Charming flew as though on wings
To fetch these necessary things,
And Uncle William ran his pen
Through 'well-beloved John,' and then
Proceeded, in the place of same,
To substitute Miss Charming's name:
Who now resides in Portman Square
And is accepted everywhere.

PETER GOOLE
WHO RUINED HIS FATHER AND MOTHER
BY EXTRAVAGANCE

Part I

Young Peter Goole, a child of nine
Gave little reason to complain.
Though an imaginative youth
He very often told the truth,
And never tried to black the eyes
Of Comrades of superior size.
He did his lessons (more or less)
Without extravagant distress,
And showed sufficient intellect,
But failed in one severe defect;
It seems he wholly lacked a sense
Of limiting the day's expense,
And money ran between his hands
Like water through the Ocean Sands.
Such conduct could not but affect
His parent's fortune, which was wrecked
Like many and many another one
By folly in a spendthrift son:
By that most tragical mischance,
An Only Child's Extravagance.

There came a day when Mr Goole
– The Father of this little fool –
With nothing in the bank at all
Was up against it, like a wall.
He wrang his hands, exclaiming, 'If
I only had a bit of Stiff
How different would be my life!'
Whereat his true and noble wife
Replied, to comfort him, 'Alas!

I said that this would come to pass!
Nothing can keep us off the rocks
But Peter's little Money Box.'
The Father, therefore (and his wife),
They prised it open with a knife –
But nothing could be found therein
Save two bone buttons and a pin.

Part II

They had to sell the house and grounds
For less than twenty thousand pounds,
And so retired, with broken hearts,
To vegetate in foreign parts,
And ended their declining years
At Blidah – which is near Algiers.
There, in the course of time, they died,
And there lie buried side by side.
While when we turn to Peter, he
The cause of this catastrophe,
There fell upon him such a fate
As makes me shudder to relate.
Just in its fifth and final year,
His University Career
Was blasted by the new and dread
Necessity of earning bread.
He was compelled to join a firm
Of Brokers – in the summer term!

And even now, at twenty-five,
He has to WORK to keep alive!
Yes! All day long from 10 till 4!
For half the year or even more;
With but an hour or two to spend
At luncheon with a city friend.

'Mamma' said Amanda 'I want to know what
  Our relatives mean when they say
That Aunt Jane is a Gorgon who ought to be shot,
  Or at any rate taken away.

'Pray what is a Gorgon and why do you shoot
  It? Or are its advances refused?
Or is it perhaps a maleficent Brute?
  I protest I am wholly bemused.'

'The Term,' said her Mother, 'is certain to pain,
  And is quite inexcusably rude.
Moreover Aunt Jane, though uncommonly plain,
  Is also uncommonly good.

'She provides information without hesitation,
  For people unwilling to learn;
And often bestows good advice upon those
  Who give her no thanks in return.

'She is down before anyone's up in the place –
  That is, up before anyone's down.
Her Domestics are awed by the shape of her face
  And they tremble with fear at her frown.

'Her visiting list is of Clergymen who
  Have reached a respectable age,
And she pays her companion MISS ANGELA DREW
  A sufficient and regular wage.

'Her fortune is large, though we often remark
  On a modesty rare in the rich;
For her nearest and dearest are quite in the dark
  As to what she will leave, or to which.

'Her conduct has ever been totally free
    From censorious whispers of ill,
At any rate, since 1903 –
    And probably earlier still.

'Your Father's dear sister presents, in a word,
    A model for all of her sex,
With a firmness of will that is never deterred,
    And a confidence nothing can vex.

'I can only desire that you too should aspire
    To such earthly reward as appears
In a high reputation, at present entire,
    After Heaven knows how many years.

'So in future remember to turn a deaf ear
    To detraction – and now run away
To your brothers and sisters whose laughter I hear
    In the garden below us at play.'

'Oh thank you, Mamma!' said Amanda at that,
    And ran off to the innocent band
Who were merrily burying Thomas the Cat
    Right up to his neck in the sand.

ON FOOD

Alas! What various tastes in food
Divide the human brotherhood!
Birds in their little nests agree
With Chinamen, but not with me.
Colonials like their oysters hot,
Their omelettes heavy – I do not.
The French are fond of slugs and frogs,
The Siamese eat puppy-dogs.
The nobles at the brilliant Court

[285]

Of Muscovy consumed a sort
Of candles held and eaten thus,
As though they were asparagus.
The Spaniard, I have heard it said,
Eats garlic, by itself, on bread:
Now just suppose a friend or dun
Dropped in to lunch at half-past one
And you were jovially to say,
'Here's bread and garlic! Peg away!'
I doubt if you would gain your end
Or soothe the dun, or please the friend.
In Italy the traveller notes
With great disgust the flesh of goats
Appearing on the table d'hôtes;
And even this the natives spoil
By frying it in rancid oil.
In Maryland they charge like sin
For nasty stuff called terrapin;
And when they ask you out to dine
At Washington, instead of wine,
They give you water from the spring
With lumps of ice for flavouring,
That sometimes kill and always freeze
The high plenipotentiaries.
In Massachusetts all the way
From Boston down to Buzzards Bay
They feed you till you want to die
On rhubarb pie and pumpkin pie,
And horrible huckleberry pie,
And when you summon strength to cry,
'What is there else that I can try?'
They stare at you in mild surprise
And serve you other kinds of pies.
And I with these mine eyes have seen
A dreadful stuff called Margarine

Consumed by men in Bethnal Green.
But I myself that here complain
Confess restriction quite in vain.
I feel my native courage fail
To see a Gascon eat a snail;
I dare not ask abroad for tea;
No cannibal can dine with me;
And all the world is torn and rent
By varying views on nutriment.
And yet upon the other hand,
De gustibus non disputand –
                              –Um.

INDEX OF FIRST LINES

[289]

Of Courtesy, it is much less: P.40
Of meadows drowsy with Trinacrian bees: P.21
Of old 'twas Samuel sought the Lord: today: P.114
Of old when folk lay sick and sorely tried: P.112
Of this bad world the loveliest and the best: P.115
Of three in One and One in three: P.113
Oh! do not play me music any more: P.10
'Oh Murder! What was that, Papa': P.267
Oh! ye that prink it to and fro: P.159
On a winter's night long time ago: P.30
On Sussex hills where I was bred: P.89
Pale Ebenezer thought it wrong to fight: P.118
Paunch talks against good liquor to excess: P.111
Pelagius lived in Kardanoel: P.90
Perkins' Duchesses have marked a great: P.111
Pugley denies the soul? Why, so do I: P.112
Remote and ineffectual Don: P.153
Rhinoceros, your hide looks all undone: P.239
Rise up, and do begin the day's adorning: P.5
Rose, little Rose, the youngest of the Roses: P.105
Sally is gone that was so kindly: P.64
Save on the rare occasions when the Sun: P.119
Shall any man for whose strong love another: P.12
She would be as the stars in your sight: P.116
Shooting one day with other people in: P.136
Sing to me of the Islands, O daughter of Cohoolin, sing: P.77
Sir Anthony Habberton, Justice and Knight: P.221
Some say that Juliet found a Friend, and some: P.104
Some time ago a tall Romantic Pole: P.137
Some years ago you heard me sing: P.276
Stand thou forever among human Houses: P.121
Stealthy the silent hours advance, and still: P.119
Strong God which made the topmost stars: P.46
Subtle – your keen analysis and nice: P.111
Suns may set and suns may rise: P.116
That which is one they shear and make it twain: P.14
The accursèd power which stands on Privilege: P.115
The Big Baboon is found upon: P.239
The Bison is vain, and (I write it with pain): P.244
The Cambrian Welsh or Mountain Sheep: P.242
The Camelopard, it is said: P.238
The cause of all the poor in '93: P.130

[294]

The world's a stage – and I'm the Super man: P.163
The world's a stage. The light is in one's eyes: P.163
The world's a stage. The trifling entrance fee: P.164
The young, the lovely and the wise: P.102
There is a light around your head: P.29
There is a literary man: P.224
There is a wall of which the stones: P.44
There is no fortress of man's flesh so made: P.100
There was a Boy whose name was Jim: P.260
There was a man called William Shand: P.219
There was a man was half a clown: P.32
There was a Queen of England: P.48
Therefore do thou, stiff-set Northumberland: P.204
These are the lawns where Cœlia lived and moved: P.118
They sell good Beer at Haslemere: P.53
They that have been beside us all the day: P.21
They that have taken wages of things done: P.15
They warned Our Lady for the Child: P.39
They whom their mothers bare through Summer heat: P.76
This Creature, though rare, is still found to the East: P.245
This diamond, Juliet, will adorn: P.117
This is the laughing-eyed amongst them all: P.5
This is the place where Dorothea smiled: P.113
This learned Fish has not sufficient brains: P.239
This man's desire; that other's hopeless end: P.116
This, the last ornament among the peers: P.114
Thou ugly, lowering, treacherous Quean: P.97
Though Man made wine, I think God made it too: P.25
Three Graces; and the mother were a Grace: P.117
Three Graces, Muses nine, of Pleiads seven: P.105
To exalt, enthrone, establish and defend: P.80
Tom had a little pony, Jack: P.278
Tonight in million-voicèd London I: P.113
Torture will give a dozen pence or more: P.111
Towards the evening of her splendid day: P.117
Two visions permanent: his native place: P.104
Two years ago, or it may be three: P.88
Verse should be set to Music. This is set: P.105
We might have heard great Homer in a hall: P.138
We rode together all in pride: P.78
We will not whisper, we have found the place: P.18
What are the names for Beauty? Who shall praise: P.16

[295]